GW00359749

Acknowledg

I would like to thank my dear wife Kathleen for her continued love and support.

My sons Pádhraic, Seán, Philip and especially my daughter Helena for help and patience in preparing the manuscript.

I owe a great deal of gratitude to my good friend Seán Kelly for his words of encouragement and for writing such a complimentary forward.

Thanks to Teresa Power whose wonderful drawings are once again featured in my book.

Thanks to all of the staff at Original Writing for their courtesy and professionalism.

Finally thank you dear reader for buying a copy of my book. I would welcome any comments you might have to *philippoet @gmail.com* or by card or letter to *Liscarroll, County Cork, Rep. of Ireland*

Philip Egan
September, 2012.

Commendations

"Just as Robert Service captured the great yarns of the gold rush in poems that were easy to remember and a joy to recite, so Philip Egan has captured in this fine collection, a strand of great Irish béaloideas tradition."
Micheál Martin Former Government Ministir and present Leader of Fianna Fáil.

Philip's collection of poetry captures the mysterious, the beautiful, the familiar, the warmth, the colour and the magic of the familiar."
Adi Roche, Director of Chernobyl Children's Project International.

"From canyons through prairies and football pitches, Philip's verse rolls on and recovers childhood."
Joseph Woods Poetry Ireland.

What other readers said:
"Your poetry has brought my poor faith a little closer to God."
"Wonderful poetry.I could read it over and over."
"Your poetry has become my prayer book and source for meditation."
"I wish people would slow down and observe the beauty of the world like in, "The Wonder of it All."

Philip Egan lives with his wife Kathleen, sons Padhráic, Séan, Philip and daughter Helena in the North Cotk village of Liscarroll. He is a dairy farmer and publican.

Touched by Rhyme: One Hundred Selected Poems is his third collection of poetry. He has been featured on the Mooney Show on Radio 1 on two occasions speaking about his poetry and philosophy in life.

Contents

A Message from Séan Kelly
M.E.P.

Now that we have a poet in the park it is appropriate and timely that we take time out to concentrate more on the remarkable power of poetry to influence, to charm and to entertain us by the power of words practised by those with such rare talents, our gifted poets.

There are few as gifted as my good friend Philip Egan. Like the great poets Dylan Thomas and Oliver Goldsmith, Philip's poetry connects with people. He connects with people; he writes about things that we know, recalls moments that we treasure and lauds heroes that we appreciate greatly. In this, Philip's latest anthology, he reaches heights of expression, description and entertainment.

As Dylan Thomas did with 'Under Milk Wood', Philip captures the characters that shaped his life around Liscarroll in his lovely classical poem 'Behold the Men I Knew Before'; his descriptions of the postman, creamery manager, butcher, school master, the merchant and so on are keenly apt and deeply emotional, especially as the simple life and years gone by slowly fade away.

Football and hurling are deeply embedded in Irish life and Philip really captures this important social phenomenon in a way few other poets have. Witness the churn of the blacksmith's forge 'disorderly but gay', as in troops a young lad with hurling, not horses, on his mind.

> And now a small boy brings his hurley round
> He wants a band put on to make it sound,
> He tells Dave all about his game tonight,
> And leaves the forge with rapture and delight.

The local hackney man was often the only connection between the village and the town. It might also be the only means to transport a team of young lads to a game. 'He fits a dozen in, leaves none behind/ They lose by seven goals, he doesn't mind.' One could write a treatise on the history and values captured in those two lines. Take the following lines:

> With skill innate and steadfast faith.
> In football pure and true,
> Why still today when men play great
> They are compared with you...

-From The Islandman four lines that capture the charm, the purity and the enduring home of the great Island man Mick O Connell, regarded by many as the greatest footballer of them all.

The anthology is rich in content and variation, poems about nature - 'the Butterfly' being a magnificent example - live long on the tongue and what about a lovely lyric about the day Philip saved the school from burning and the school master from the wrath of the visiting inspector. The heater caught fire as the inspector examined the pupils, but our brave Philip and his class mates saved the day and the school:

'We Threw water on the heater and water on the wall/ And water on the inspector which was the best of all'; bravo! And bravo to Philip for capturing such rare moments in such a witty and charming way.

Yes, this is a beautiful anthology - endearing, witty and entertaining. God has bestowed us with 'a talent rare and true', our great poet Philip Egan. Maybe we should prepare for him to take over in Áras an Uachtaráin from the poet in the park, Micheal D. President Philip the Poet sounds very good to me.

Congratulations Philip and Best Wishes,

Sean Kelly
1st August 2012

Also by the same author:

Rhymes from the Homestead
Rhymes for a Starry Night

******

"I know a russet gate that's hanging upside down
It leads me to the laneway of my dreams,
Half a mile from heaven and half a mile from town
And half a mile from ever rolling streams."

From

Laneway of Dreams
Rhymes from the Homestead.
Philip Egan.

****

"Daddy and Mammy help me please
Your boy is in need of repose,
I hear you calling through the breeze
But God there's that pain in my toes,
I'll try to snuggle down to sleep
But Mammy where is my pillow?
The bench is hard and I can't keep
My sore eyes fixed on tomorrow."

From

On a Parkside Bench
Rhymes for a Starry Night.
Philip Egan.

****

For my son Philip.

Bobby and Me and Mick O' Dea

Bobby and me and Mick O'Dea were friends right from the
start,
From the first day when we did play we seldom were apart,
Out in the street when we would meet the three of us would go
To hilltops green where we were seen in sunshine, rain and
snow.
Oh it was good to know I could depend on those two chums,
For side by side we were allied in brawls and scrapes and scrums,
When Bob was cut I ran barefoot to help him o'er the glade,
And Mick in truth once lost a tooth when he came to my aid.

While up in school our golden rule was help each other out,
I whispered loud with my head bowed when Bobby was in
doubt,
The bamboo cane drew instant pain; we took three in each hand
Our hands were fried, we seldom cried, still taller we did stand.
Out in the yard 'twas always hard to pick one o'er the other
 For both were true as sky is blue and each was like a brother,
If Bob was fast then Mick could blast the ball with speed and
verve
And still defend until the end, a slim lead to preserve.

We often rode and always showed true courage on the trail,
Upon his steed Bob saw the need to guard the midday mail,
At break of dawn we would be gone from our outpost out west,
And Bobby knew when the wind blew which trail was trickiest.

While Mick O'Dea from up a tree could shoot a bandit dead
And he would shout (I'd flatten out), "Hey, boys, don't spare the
lead!"
Behind a rock we would take stock of bandits all around
We'd shoot them all and they would fall like fleas down on the
ground.

In the ball court we played for sport each evening after school,
My right was bad, Mick's left was sad, together we did rule,
I'd toss an ace, Mick pushed the pace, we were the best in class
At twenty all we'd make a call and hit a shot to pass.
But Bob was best, indeed was blessed at half a mile or more,
I saw him run straight from the gun, win races by the score,
When the bell went he got the scent of victory throughout,
He'd hear the cheer and up a gear, the whole field he would
rout.

Though love is great I lost a mate and then I lost the other,
They left the town where we put down great days and nights
together,
Mick worked his tricks, made goals with flicks for his adopted
team,
Reached heady heights on summer nights and realised his
dream.
On the rail track Bob did not lack great skill and expertise,
With sleepers great he helped create the railway line at ease,
Out in the dark he'd often mark the track for quick repair,
He'd walk a mile, I guess would smile and see a bandit there.

I stayed behind for I was blind to green hills far away,
But still I see those chums with me when I walk out each day,
They sometimes call, they still enthral with tales of long ago,
Why, Bobby said that I was dead, the day we rode through snow.
Far wiser men more deft with pen you'll meet than us three souls,
But memories are such as these, we guarded the payrolls,
When times were rough and men were tough you could count on us three,
Yes Bob was great, a super mate, and so was Mick O' Dea.

Preview to next Poem

The following poem or piece could have been written about any village in Ireland during the period when I grew up in the nineteen sixties.

In the village of Liscarroll in North Cork where I grew up, there were 17 houses at either side of the street. Twenty of those houses were occupied as business premises of one type or other. Today half a century later just five houses have in them a business. Most of the adult population of our village during my childhood were born in the early part of the twentieth century. Many of them lived through every notable event in the history of the state. Most of them grew up in an Ireland before super stores, motor cars, telephones, and televisions were freely available and before agriculture became intensive. All of them knew hardship when money and provisions were scarce and hard to come by.

As a young boy I met them at every corner and every twist and turn. They gathered in the street each night for chat and banter. They were loved, respected, feared and admired, all in equal measure. However, they all had one thing in common: they were hard working and decent people who played a significant part in the development of the new state.

I would like to dedicate Behold the Men I Knew Before to the following men who helped to shape our village and our country with their hard work and foresight,

BEHOLD THE MEN I KNEW BEFORE
August 1963

The morning chorus greets the break of day
The gluttonous old fox is on his way,
The sober herd move closer to the gate
Where patiently and quietly they wait,
The villagers sleep on for one more hour
Then they wake with blossom and with flower,
And greet the sunshine soaking up the dew
In meadows where the fuchsia is in view.

1. THE POSTMAN

Oh blessed is he who brings the letters 'round
At half past six in the Post Office found,
And sorting the mail that arrived today
From loved ones with post stamps from far away,
A wise man dressed in uniform to fit
He reads his books at night and does profit,
In better times with education true
In the Senate or Dáil he could argue,
But now while on his rounds in native tongue
He rouses up the old, inspires the young,
Gives bullseyes and clove rocks to children small
Then trips over a leg, pretends to fall,
Today as he pedals up the boreen
The lilacs and the daisies are serene,
He whistles an old tune that brings him joy
A parcel for the widow and her boy.

2. The Creamery Manager

Upon the creamery stand with jolly face
The manager each morning takes his place,
Well enlightened with a first class degree
He serves as advisor and referee,
He gazes o'er the glasses on his nose
And tastes the milk at random as it flows,
Quite discreet with the message he relays
Forbearance with small farmers he displays,
Even children love the warmth of his smile
He winks at them with mischief to beguile,
Yes he is kind and if he has a sin
It is his love of football there within,
Across the county bounds he likes to pass
On sunny Sundays after second mass,
Back to his native village all are told
Where first he learned to love the green and gold.

3. THE BUILDER

The truck is loaded up, it's time to go
Ten men are in the back, 'tis quite a show,
This is not Camden Town or Cricklewood
But Buckley's yard where employment is good,
A lively man Tom takes it in his stride
Changing the face of Ireland's countryside,
Where once were roofs of sheet iron and of and thatch
There now are roofs of slate with doors to match,
A hurling man in nineteen thirty-four
A county medal won when green he wore,
And still he keeps the village flag afloat
By keeping twenty workmen from the boat,
Back in the truck there is great fun and cheer
As the town of Kildorrery draws near,
The road is rough and as the men alight
They curse the porter that they drank last night.

4. THE BUTCHER

Behold the tallest man in the fair street
In his small shop you easily can greet,
A gentleman 'tis said that on a tray
He brings breakfast to his wife every day,
Oh sharp is he at adding in his head
While filling boxes up with jam and bread,
And if by chance he plucks his pencil down
He tots up twenty things on paper brown,
A humorist he is to all the mums
Until at three a butcher he becomes,
Today the man within him is alive
While cutting up pork chops he seems to thrive,
The customers say strength he does not lack
While hanging salty bacon on a rack,
But still they gaze and still they wonder how
Upon his back he carries half a cow.

5. The Ironmonger

The floorboards creak along the corridor
Between the kitchen and the hardware store,
For the impatient one it seems an age
Before the ironmonger comes onstage,
He whistles a sweet tune on his way out
Sells balls of twine, at night time pints of stout,
The shop is dark and eerie, not a sound
But in this store the finest pikes are found,
And shovels too for workmen on the road
Milk buckets guaranteed not to corrode.
The woman with the shawl wants paraffin
Weekly she calls and gives two bottles in,
The paraffin is wrapped in Thursday's news
But no one sees her taking home the booze,
The paraffin will keep her lamp aglow
The whiskey small comforts to her bestow.

6. The Council Worker

He brushes the pavement as best he can
Today he is a broken hearted man,
He has buried the son that he loves so
In the small cemetery down below,
Now back at work is hard as hard can be
He takes a neighbour's handshake graciously,
He finds that he can't talk about the day
An accident took his small boy away,
He thinks about the others still not grown
Knowing too well he is their cornerstone,
So daily with his shovel and his brush
He sweeps the road and trims back verge and bush,
But he just cannot raise his spirits high
For everywhere he sees his laughing boy.
In two weeks the village will mourn once more
A daddy joins his son on heaven's shore.

7. The Coalman

The coalman is indebted to his cob
With awkwardness he murmurs, "Come on, Bob,"
With one hand he has loaded up his cart
His aged mother tells him to depart,
No ordinary man 'tis a great feat
To deliver the coal around the street,
Way back in time a young boy was laid low
And still carries the scars of polio,
With one hand in the belt behind his back
The other lifts the coal out every sack,
Great courage and willpower he daily shows
As up and down the village street he goes,
A young boy passing by lends him a hand
And shovels in the coal at his command,
He scoops a handful out and tips the scales
The bags are loaded up above the rails.

8. THE SCHOOL TEACHER

Over the hill the village master rules
In this the most good spirited of schools,
With desks inscribed with names now far away
And maps up on the wall now in decay,
Today the class the master has called 'round
For adding sums with answers to astound,
The master knows the middling from the good
Helps lesser mortals to a livelihood,
Helps every boy to pick and catch and call
And solo up the wing with a football,
A quiet man he serves his country great
By passing on its customs and its faith,
And poetry and some say Latin prose
From manuscripts the village master knows,
Oh wise is he and in the evening time
He profits from his garden and his rhyme.

9. THE GARDENER

By the race course where point to points are run
A plot of ground that is second to none,
Here the finest potatoes can be got
And cabbage that is ready for the pot,
Or lettuce to adorn a salad dish
On summer evenings with a tasty fish,
The gardener with rake and hoe and spade
Tends daily to the furrows he has made.
At noon a young boy calls for rhubarb sticks
Is startled by the pen knife that he flicks,
Down on his knees he cuts the stumps away
The young boy talks of this for half the day,
The gardener talks nonsense to bemuse
And wraps the rhubarb in yesterday's news,
For the young family down in the street
Rhubarb and custard is a weekly treat.

10. THE UNDERTAKER

The undertaker has learned well his trade
For fifty years fine coffins he has made,
The shavings are all scattered on the floor
Of the small shed outside the kitchen door,
This portly man is jolly and humane
Works easy with his chisel and his plane,
The coffin on the block is taking shape
He measures top to bottom with his tape,
The elders of the village call around
With knowledge great on racing horse and hound,
They pass the time and light up for a smoke
One orders his own coffin made of oak,
The undertaker shows him one to fit
Then jokingly demands a deposit,
These aged men full of the joys of life
In their time have known poverty and strife.

11. The Pensioner

Behold the castle in the village grand
The finest to be seen in all the land,
Stately it beckons to folk passing by
Who gaze at it with an enquiring eye,
No more it flinches from the cannon's roar
No soldiers lying wounded on the floor,
Where once it was a fortress of the great
It is now a monument of the state,
Today two young boys scale the castle walls
An old man sees the danger and he calls,
With devilment they disappear from view
At fourteen years the dangers they are few,
For centuries above this ancient town
The castle walls with dignity look down,
The young boys climb the walls and then they grow
Into manhood in their own place below.

12. The Newsagent

Oh wise is he who reads the daily news
Before the mass goers have left their pews,
A chemist it is said he could have been
Now in the paper shop he sets the scene,
And opens up for sixteen hours a day
A marathon in truth for modest pay,
The villagers vouch for his earnest smile
It is as forthcoming in the last mile,
The evening bus pulls in but few alight
The weekly comics are dropped off tonight,
A box of newborn chicks duly arrive
Up in the cottage plot they'll surely thrive,
A young boy buys his Beano, steals a glance
At other comics when he gets the chance,
Yes all year round this is the late, late show
In memory the paper shop will glow.

13. The Lorry Driver

From Ballybeg a lorry load of lime
Travels the roads of Munster all the time,
John Scanell is the pilot at the wheel
At every town a pint of stout will steal,
The truck travels along at tortoise pace
As John peers out with lime on hair and face,
"She'll never forgive us if we pass by,"
He tells his co-pilot who won't belie,
And so they stop for a pint and a drop
Before they carry on to their next stop.
Back home they say at handball he has flair
Though he never takes the time to prepare,
He prefers to sit up on a high stool
A man at ease, unexcited and cool.
Lucky are they who taste his charm and wit
Or who beside him at a card game sit.

14. The Farmer and Farm Worker

Sweet tastes the currant bread and cups of tea
At evening time in meadows heavenly,
The farmer and his neighbours gathered 'round
In fellowship and loyalty profound,
Small children jumping over cocks of hay
The tired old dog panting out of the way,
The young boy pulling buts with tender hands
The farm-hand turning swards in the headlands,
It's eight o'clock, the cows now leave the stall
The farmhand heads off home, he can recall
Going into service while still a boy
Not for him an easy life filled with joy,
But still he dreams and helps his mum each night
Plays for the village team and does excite,
One day he will excel at handball too
And chair the County Board with balanced view.

15. THE POSTMASTER

Upon his bike young Michael pedals hard
Up Altamira hill to the farm yard,
A telegram he has and it will pay
A penny if there is good news today,
A banker he will be at twenty-one
Today he is being a helpful son,
His family who served the village well
Now take a break with many tales to tell.
Up at O'Cáinte's shop the post will stay
For half a century from this fair day,
Young Donal in his time will see much change
But first his mother's shop must rearrange,
He talks of Pearce and Tone and Ireland's great
Is helped around the shop by Auntie Kate,
From this historic house a mother's son
As president will be second to none.

16. The Blacksmith

Beside the crossroads bar that points the way
The blacksmith's forge disorderly but gay,
Just now a good horse is brought to be shod
Soon on the fields and byways he will plod,
Two brothers, Dave and Pat work in the dark
They stoke up the dead fire to find a spark,
These gentle souls both like to work at ease
And come and go to duty as they please,
While Dave enjoys a pint across the way
His brother Pat shoes up the dapple grey,
The sparks fly now inside the blacksmith's door
And charmed is he, who hears the bellows roar,
And now a small boy brings his hurley 'round
He wants a band put on to make it sound,
He tells Dave all about his game tonight
And leaves the forge with rapture and delight.

17. The Shopkeeper

A purveyor of spirits, wine and tea
He sits behind the counter quietly,
And gazes through the window of his shop
While sucking on a lemon lollipop,
Like a sentry he knows the ins and outs
Of village life, the people's fears and doubts,
Free sweets he gives to children when they call
Maybe a few pence off a windy ball.
Tomorrow in the kitchen he must dwell
And tot the ledger for his clientele,
Credit he gives to those who are in need
He knows the house where there are kids to feed,
Some people pay just once or twice a year
His wife thinks he is not a great cashier,
Half a century later folk will say
That he fed half the village in his day.

18. The Priest

It's evening time, the church is near half full
The congregation devout and prayerful,
At benediction all are called to grace
There is great peacefulness about the place,
The priest is reciting the rosary
Flanked by ten boys in the sanctuary,
A pious man, he's been here fifteen years
Tonight he's fighting to hold back the tears,
The bishop has told him it's time to go
He tells his brethren in the pews below,
He has been the heartbeat of village life
The confidant of husband and of wife,
The young boys wearing sutans at his side
He has baptised with water purified,
With heavy heart he sings the final hymn
And grown men there shed tears as well as him.

19. THE FREEDOM FIGHTER

"Fearless, faithful and true," the old men say
Of him who fought for freedom in his day,
And now he is a hero far and wide
And freely walks his village street with pride,
But still there is a teardrop in his eye
Why did so many comrades have to die?
And flashbacks he surely gets now and then
Of life when on the run with fighting men,
This evening he goes to a handball game
In the ball court that soon will bear his name,
When he arrives two men turn on the style
Sometimes austere, he manages a smile,
Tomorrow on the train he has to go
With farming men for milk prices are low,
The man who risked his life for freedom's cause
Now fights for farmer's rights to great applause.

20. The Hackney Driver

In this old town the motor cars are few
But Larry Coleman has bought one brand new,
A hackney man he is known far and wide
The money that he earns is justified,
A pregnant mum at three knocks on his door
Exhausted she collapses on the floor,
Just out of bed he reassures her now
And gets her to the hospital somehow,
It's five o' clock before his day is done
She's smiling now and with her newborn son,
This evening he gets ready for a match
But knows the youngsters are not up to scratch,
He fits a dozen in, leaves none behind
They lose by seven goals, he doesn't mind,
He tells them one and all their day will come
They fall out in the street like in a scrum.

21. The Barber

The barber puts a board up on the chair
For the young boy so he can cut his hair,
By day he is a ganger on the road
At evening time he cuts hair in one mode,
Not for him the fashions of Liverpool
The Beatles would be sheared if on his stool,
And so he clips with vigour to the bone
The young boy is bewildered on his throne,
Upon the walls of this small sitting room
Are cuttings of great sportsmen in full bloom,
The young boy looks around and takes in all
He's transfixed by one photo on the wall,
A picture of the Busby Babes that died
The day the master in the classroom cried,
The barber will be resting in fine clay
When that young boy will write of him one day.

22. The Confectioner

Near the sweet shop at one end of the street
In great comradeship natives nightly meet,
And on the flagstones there play pitch and toss
Or hit a ball against the wall across,
Up in the air you'll see the pennies twirl
And teased is he, who compliments a girl,
Here you will hear tall yarns and quips galore
And luscious are the sweets inside the store,
There's lucky bags that have in soldier men
And jelly babies sold by the dozen,
Or toffee bars that would loosen a tooth
The men outside have lost most in their youth,
Tonight they sit and joke with thoughts expressed
About a hurling game they have witnessed
The pitch and toss, the banter to upstage
Defines the entertainment of an age.

23. The Mechanic

The man from way back west works hard and long
Here in the village now he does belong,
He dreams about a garage of his own
But first he must dig out the rock and stone,
With pick and shovel and crowbar to grind
Quite steady grows the mound that he has mined,
The perspiration runs down from his face
As each day he creates a bit more space,
He draws away the stone that he has cut
With the loan of a neighbour's horse and butt,
The work is hard; some say he won't succeed
But men from way back west are a tough breed,
At ten o'clock he soothes his grubby hands
Tomorrow there will be greater demands
This is a feat strong men would boast about
He pours himself a small bottle of stout.

24. The Labourer

The Polish man is struggling to survive
In this small town he finds it hard to thrive,
He travels far for work on his push bike
Prepared to take a pick-axe or a pike,
"The wages are too low," he tells Maureen
The local girl that he took as his queen,
Their seven children are tucked up in bed
It doesn't last them long, a loaf of bread,
The tears roll down his face in that small room
The eldest boy awake senses the gloom,
In two months time they will be on a ship
Bound for New Zealand on an awesome trip,
Out in the street they sell before they go
Their few possessions in a sad, sad show,
There's heartbreak when they leave their dog behind
A young boy takes their rabbit home to mind.

25. The Publican

Next to the old barracks on the Main Street
The village pub where nightly locals meet,
And here good men and fair men have a view
On everything from sport to revenue,
The proprietor is frank and sincere
More at ease with his cows than filling beer,
A prayerful man it is true to relate
At solving mathematics he is great,
Like the postman he too in better days
Would have designed great houses and railways,
But as landlord he finds it hard to bear
The tittle-tattle of the dozen there,
Though tonight all agree on Father Dan
A devout and God-fearing holy man,
The publican treads wearily to bed
The tittle-tattle spinning in his head.

26. The Guard

Near the Bog Cross where once a robber fled
The guard patrols tonight kind spirited,
A decent man his passion is to play
A game of cards and back a horse each day,
Unaffected by the uniform he wears
Great warmness with the villagers he shares,
And compassion for those of lesser means
Good counsel and intelligence he gleans,
Applies it for the benefit of all
Far better to advise before the fall,
The broken man, the beggar gone astray
Beyond the midnight hour have passed this way,
Just before he ends his guardianship
In a whisper he is given a tip,
Back home he checks the runners for next day
The Shinning One he will bet on each way.

Beneath the moon that lights the summer sky
The castle walls are soothing to the eye,
They cast a steadfast arm around the place
Invite the passer-by footsteps to trace,
It's past midnight, the village sleeps once more
While dreaming of a better life in store,
The wily fox, the badger and the owl
In woodland, furze and gorse are on the prowl.

Why Ned Dawley Missed
The Dance

'Twas in the ballroom of romance Ned Dawley met his bride,
He courted her at every chance around the countryside,
To picture halls and shooting stalls he took her by the arm,
And bragged about the grand layout he had down at the farm.
He loved her so that he did go to great trouble to date
The dainty lass who had got class and raised up his pulse rate,
Aye night and day he made his way along the small boreen
To be beside his future bride the beautiful Maureen.

Though Ned could pull or fight a bull he carried two left feet
And in the ballroom of romance his dancing was not sweet,
When waltzing round he always found it a cause of distress
In case he'd stand or even land on top of Maureen's dress.
He couldn't jive, when he'd arrive with Maureen on the floor
He'd only shake and she would make a beeline for the door,
It was a cause of strain because she loved to cut a dash
Inside the hall or at a ball or any kind of bash.

Said she to Ned whose face was red, "You'll have to get some
spunk
And learn to jive and look alive rather than looking drunk,
Next Sunday night you'll be a sight inside the village hall
If you can't whirl with your own girl at the Duhallow Ball."
He scratched his head, "There won't," he said, "be anyone as
quick

At jigs and reels or kicking heels or any other trick,
I have a week in which to peak, I'll be like Fred Astaire,
Maureen, my dear, come over here and kiss your Teddy Bear".

He hatched a plan next morning ran excited to the stall,
With milking done he kept in one cow to help for the Ball,
Now Josephine was quite serene in parlour, yard or shed,
"You'll do for now, my lovely cow," the bold Ned Dawley said,
While in the bail he caught her tail and jived with skills anew,
With music high he reached the sky and like a sparrow flew,
"By Gosh," said he, "I know I'll be a credit to Maureen
All thanks to you, my lovely moo, good on you, Josephine."

Thus there inside the stall he tried all kinds of skips and dance
While the good beast seemed in the least bit troubled by this
prance,
All of that week he chose to seek the good cow for tuition,
'Twas worth his while for with some style his dreams came to
fruition,
With hope re-born then came the morn' of the Duhallow Ball,
The aged cow was weary now of living in the stall,
The music too upset the moo 'twas blaring o'er her head,
"Tonight's the night now you sit tight," to her Ned Dawley said.

Before he'd go and steal the show with Maureen his own girl,
In his best suit, Ned did salute the cow for one last whirl,
Deprived of grass the kindly lass was in no form for jiving,
He caught her tail; she pulled the bail and sent Ned Dawly flying.
While on the ground alarmed he found the cow's tail was held
high,
In a great spurt upon his shirt, Josephine did let fly,
His suit was ruined and he was doomed, he sat there in a trance,
And that is why with fury high Ned Dawley missed the dance.

The Day We Saved the School

It wasn't me or Mick O'Dea who caused all the hubbub
But Whacker who was quite handy at fixing tank or tub,
The oil heater just would not light so he took it apart
The master stood there all polite knowing it had to start.
Well it was cold there in the room on that November day
And all of us sat in the gloom; it was too wet to play,
There was a smell of paraffin from Whacker on the floor
When suddenly who walked straight in but the damn inspector.

The master looked on in a trance, his face as white as snow
And then I saw it change colour to a bright reddish glow,
We scurried on down to our seats, like little lambs afraid
I swear that there were missed heartbeats while we sat there and
prayed.
The master took his scarf and coat and hung them on a rack
He had a whisker like a goat, a belly like a sack,
With eyes that pierced the rimless specs that hung upon his nose
He stood and stared at twenty wrecks all sullen and morose.

"Come tell me, boys," said he with pride, "Who is De Valera?"
And Scrapper Browne right quick replied, "The President of
Eire,"
"Now who," said he, "is Pádraig Pearse? Someone put up his
hand,"
Said Dodger Hayes, "With fighting fierce he died to save Ireland."

"On what river would you find Cork?" he then asked Mick O'
Dea
And Mick replied fast as a hawk, "Sir, Cork is on the Lee."
We were doin' well and we could tell the master was right proud
But Shorty Jones when his turn came just stood with his head
bowed.

The Whacker had the heater fixed albeit with great haste
And with all of his heroics he was black to the waist,
The master called the inspector and sat him by the fire
But he was still a tormentor with questions that were dire.
"Can anybody tell me where the river Shannon flows?"
And we just stared into thin air, said I, "Nobody knows,"
"Alright," said he, "where would you pass a winkers that's thread
bare?"
The Whacker roared, "Upon an ass at Castleisland fair."

Well we all laughed when Buster Hayes let off a great hiccup
The Inspector looked up with rage and told us to stand up,
We sang for him 'The Minstrel Boy' with gusto and good cheer
And then said he with little joy, "Young man come over here,"
Well I was glad for this I mused was my best chance to shine
At verse or rhyme I'd be enthused, my actions were divine,
Then he gave me a cane of chalk and asked me do a sum
But all that I could do was gawk; I felt a proper bum.

I saw the master make a sign I couldn't understand
And as I wrote the number nine the chalk fell from my hand,
Just then there was a woeful bang, the heater was on fire

And from the blackboard there I sprang like a bull through barb-wire,
The inspector was on his butt as I ran out the door
And found a bucket in the hut, soon there were boys galore,
We threw water on the heater and water on the wall
And water on the inspector, which was the best of all.

We saved the school from burning down, we were heroes that day
 I was saved from looking a clown when that spark got away,
The inspector had quite enough and soon was on the road
And Dodger said he caught a cough and was fit to explode,
The Whacker was an absentee while we were on the mop
Then the master came down to me with a sweet lollipop,
"Three cheers," said he, "for all of you who got me off the hook,"
 I took the cue, "Three cheers," said I and the old classroom shook.

THE BUBBLE

A little bubble once grew tired
Of living in the sea,
Quite passionately it aspired
To be off floating free,
So day and night it hatched a plan
To ride in to the shore,
And leave forever the ocean
Float free forever more.

The little bubble found a swell
And jumped up on its back,
Oh it was bold and it fared well
 Courage it did not lack,
The swell turned into a great wave
That rolled in to the shore,
The bubble fell, 'twas a close shave
Swept back to sea once more.

And many times the bubble tried
And many times it failed,
But vowed it would not be denied
Whatever was entailed,
"I must be patient now," it said
"Wait for the summer breeze
That soon over the sea will spread
And then my chance I'll seize."

The summer came and sunshine too
And all along the shore
The bubble saw come into view
Small children by the score,
"Tomorrow I will leave," it mused
"On waves of froth I'll ride,
Soon I will be free," it enthused
"Above the countryside."

The morning came and it was bright
The breeze roused up a swell,
The bubble vowed that by moonlight
It would be free and well,
Upon the swell it pitched and tossed
And rode in towards the shore,
And many bubbles there were lost
At sea forever more.

The bubble was now in a spin
The swell was now a wave,
The wave came close to crashing in
To a gigantic cave,
"Oh no!" the little bubble cried
"This is the end for me,"
But then the wave broke up beside
The shore and set it free.

The young bubble looked all around
And saw ten thousand more
Small bubbles struggling on the ground
Along by the seashore,
"Oh gosh!" it cried "how can this be?
My friends are fading fast,
Oh it was safer in the sea
How long more can I last?"

But it was made of sterner stuff
And weaved its way among
The many bubbles which were tough
But still did not live long,
"I must get free, I must get free"
The little bubble cried,
Oh! Sand please do not shrivel me
I'm too young to be fried."

Just then it heard a gentle voice
"Oh! Bubble are you lost?
Come I will raise you up, rejoice
There isn't any cost,"
A little girl then raised it up
And gently blew it free,
The bubble saw a chimney top
And it cried out with glee…

"Oh! I am free of wind and wave
I'm happy as I go,
No longer will I be a slave
To the rough sea below,
Too long I've stayed down in the swell
But now I'm in the sky,
On clouds of happiness I'll dwell
With bird and butterfly."

.

GOD'S CHOSEN ONES

My fish are swimming oh so gay
And lively on this summer's day,
And it is with such great delight
I watch them like a bird excite,
Perky they are in water pure
In a cow trough in my pasture,
Yea this is no aquarium
But all the same is my sanctum.

It stirs my heart to watch them rise
Up to the top with equipoise,
Then with a splash they're back below
And swimming swiftly to and fro,
They fascinate me as I stare
And lost in thought I'm unaware
Of time and space as moments pass,
Of cattle grazing on the grass.

Look now, an old cow comes to drink
She stops and stares and seems to think,
I must be careful how I go
For my small friends are down below,
The fish, the cow on nature's sod
Do you think they represent God?
The fish so pure and full of grace
The cow so humble round the place.

Soft Shower

It seemed to come out of the blue
The rain that fell this morn,
And on the meadow cast a hue
Of golden to adorn.

It was as soft as morning rain
Should be in summer bliss,
Just like the bubbling of champagne
For newly weds to kiss.

And as I sheltered in the shade
A drop fell on my brow,
And then I knew that it had made
Its own refuge somehow.

For when I looked up at the trees
They soaked up in the sun
Raindrops as pure as honey bees
Or children having fun.

'Twas a soft shower filled with grace
And it was plain to see,
The raindrops and the trees embrace
In perfect harmony.

Sweet Daisy

Sweet daisy of the longest day
How glorious is your display,
In pasture green and vale and ditch
I see you lately make your pitch,
With elegance and grace for sure
And majesty for my pleasure,
You beautify the days of June
With grandeur that is opportune.

Sweet daisy of the twilight hour
Sleep softly my pretty flower,
Gently you flutter in the breeze
While I am praying on my knees,
And thanking God for pretty things
(A flower like you comfort brings),
Oh it is great in summer haze
To sit with you awhile and gaze.

Sweet daisy of my childhood dreams
I picked you out near sparkling streams,
And brought you home with pride and joy
To mother when I was a boy,
But now it seems so far away
When I was that young lad at play,
Sweet daisy of my memory
Come lift you head in victory.

THE HEROES OF TULACH LÉIS

(The Heroes of Tullylease)

In ancient times devout men came
To Tulach Léis and prayed,
'Twas long before the native game
Of hurling was displayed,
They came and said "look here is pure
With forest, vale and stream,"
They wanted Christ's words to endure
They wanted too to dream.

Around the hill they built their huts
Where they did kneel and pray,
From the large tree they gathered nuts
To count the passing day,
They sat to think and meditate
Observe the beauty found,
And on the rock and on the slate
They wrote of man and hound.

From the fresh water pure and clear
They filled their cups each morn,
In the same water year by year
They baptised the newborn,
Those holy men came to the stream
In thanksgiving to God,
For purified they found their dream
In rock and pine and sod.

When Bericheart the sainted one
Called friends around his bed,
He whispered that his work was done
Then gently bowed his head,
And as they laid his soul to rest
They felt a pleasant glow,
The holy monks knew they were blessed
And blessings did bestow.

Long centuries of growth passed by
Before the hurling game
Was played in fields to dignify
The place from where folk came,
In Tulach Léis the red and white
Was close to every heart,
And words that fuelled the appetite
Pray well to Bericheart.

In fifty-eight some bold men said
"'Tis time to plant the seed
Of victory that soon will spread
Just like our race and creed,"
They practised hard, they practised long
And won Duhallow's crown,
Now well acclaimed in verse and song
Their camáns weren't put down.

Now it is said in the Hind's Stone
The hind did leave her milk,
Provided she was left alone
That same was rich as silk,
To feed the poor was her delight
Until that beauty queen
Was disturbed and put into flight
Never more to be seen.

Around that stone in fifty–nine
The team gathered before
They made a promise to refine
Their hurling skills once more,
In fifty-nine and sixty-one
In games they talk of still,
Two more Duhallow crowns were won
With strength and speed and will.

And to the Abbey Grounds all went
And danced into the night,
The stonework there magnificent,
The sliotar in full flight!
The Dancing Master was recalled
The Hind's Stone and the deer,
And Bericheart would be enthralled
To hear his name held dear.

Alas! A barren spell came round
That great team's day had passed,
But still down in the field were found
Young men strong and steadfast,
Ten times they marched behind the band
Ten times to bend the knee,
Ten times they answered the command
"Get up play well and free!"

In zero-eight the team once more
Marched with their hearts on fire,
Two twenty-two that team did score
To fulfil their desire,
And as the cup was held up high
Some spoke of fifty-eight,
But no one present could deny
This hurling team was great.

In Tulach Léis each February
Crowds kneel at Saint Ben's well,
And some recite the rosary
And some strange tales will tell,
The aura of the holy monks
Is still close to the heart,
And on the grass and on tree-trunks
All pray to Bericheart.

A LEGEND

They sing of legends that were great
On track, on field, in ring,
And on bar-stools there is debate
On who was the darling
Of centre-court, on grass, on clay,
On bike in Tour De France,
And every legend has his day
By design and by chance.

But let me sing of Markie Stokes
Who played for thirty years,
The most congenial of blokes
Who knew more tears than cheers,
In nine Duhallow finals played
And lost the bloody lot,
From Tullylease he never strayed
Stayed loyal to that spot.

Kelly and Roche were mighty men
George Best, Delaney too,
And surely we are beholden
To Cody and his crew,
But raise a glass for a great bloke
Who helped to fan the flame,
And many a good hurley broke
All for his native game.

The Whacker

When boys wore trousers to the knee
Had legs like trunks and brown,
Wore hand me downs that were shabby
The Whacker came to town.

The Whacker joined us in our school
One fine September day,
Without a pencil, book or rule
He said he'd come to stay,
With face as red as Santa's clothes
He came and sat with me,
He used his sleeve to wipe his nose
For he had no hankie.

The Whacker was a frightful lad
For dodging school and class,
An air of devilment he had
He could be bold as brass,
Up on the wall he'd shoot a fly
With an elastic band,
But in the yard you could rely
On him to lend a hand.

When e'er he sat down on his seat
He scribbled on the desk,
And though his initials were neat
His writing was grotesque,

He couldn't spell, perhaps not tell
The seasons of the year,
But he would go for you to hell
And come back without fear.

At every fair from Cork to Clare
The Whacker struck a deal,
He'd sell a donkey, buy a mare
Even a cart or wheel,
A pot of brass he once did pass
Off as a pot of gold,
And next week when he came to class
The dosh he made was told.

The master knew his wilful ways
For wise and bold was he,
He tried to teach him on the days
He sat for poetry,
But rhyme or verse he could not tell
His feet were ill at ease,
But to a wise man he could sell
A rain drop in the breeze.

One day for Castleisland fair
The Whacker played truant,
He took a piebald donkey there
His lingo was fluent,
And up and down the thoroughfare
He showed off the fine ass

With stalls and hawkers everywhere
A sparrow could not pass.

Such crowds were rarely ever seen
Around the town before,
And on the square and village green
Were donkeys by the score,
'Twas hard to sell, as evening fell
The Whacker was on edge,
He cursed the dealers there to hell
For their lack of knowledge.

Then through the crowd steadfast and proud
The master did appear,
"Whacker," said he in tone out loud
"The donkeys are quite dear,
How much do you want for the ass?"
Asked the master in jest,
"Far better you were up in class
Doing your English test."

"'Tis kind of you to show concern,"
The Whacker answered back,
"Fifteen smackers I will not spurn
For the shirt off my back,
But surely, Sir, you only bluff
Or else I am a fool,
For you already have enough
Fine donkeys up in school."

Autogiro

I'm squashed and trampled in the crowd
A half crown in my pocket,
The bookies are calling out loud
It's evens on The Rocket,
My uncle's horse is in the race
And I am here to follow,
He's ten to one around the place,
I'm backing Autogiro.

I bet the lot and now I'm broke
He'd better end up winning,
Hope my uncle will pull a stroke
He says the horse is flying,
I'm like a punter in the crowd
With my race card and biro,
The bookies are calling out loud
Ten to one Autogiro.

They're in the ring, he looks smashing
Thanks to my Uncle Jimmy,
I hope he won't end up falling
Or I'll lose every penny,
Ferdie gets up and takes his crop
He rides with fire and gusto,
I pray to God that he won't flop
Or fall off Autogiro.

They pass the stand the first time round
He's settled in the middle,
It doesn't matter 'bout the ground
He's as fit as a fiddle,
He rises to an obstacle
As strong as a tornado,
He surely is a spectacle
When jumping, Autogiro.

But now, as they go down the back
He seems to get a wobble,
And Ferdie Roche is off his back
And clutching to the saddle,
I'm thinking that my half a crown
Is gone with none to follow,
But Ferdie will not be brought down
He's back on Autogiro.

They're in the straight, he's in the lead
And battling with The Rocket,
The whips are out, he's gaining speed
I'm clinging to my docket,
They're at the line and by a neck
He wins, the plucky fellow,
And Uncle Jimmy's there to check
His hero Autogiro.

So now we're home and I am rich
There's turkey on the table,
And Auntie Vera turns the switch
The new TV is stable,
The sports man says for Stephen's Day
The race results will follow,
We all jump up and shout hurrah
When he calls Autogiro.

Ah memories will never fade
Of my dear Uncle Jimmy,
Who over many a decade
Trained horses with mastery,
And in mind's eye I can see still
That small boy with a biro,
Marking his card in winter's chill
Good on you Autogiro,
Three cheers for Autogiro!

"Mick O Connell remains to this day the model of perfection in Gaelic Football."

Pádraig Puirséal 1979.

I always knew that some day I would visit Valentia Island, the home of Gaelic Football legend Mick O' Connell. So in the summer of 2010 I made that long awaited visit. The clock was set in my hotel room for 8 am. when I planned to rise and visit the old homestead where he practiced as a boy. For some strange reason I was already sitting on the ditch outside the house when I looked at my watch. It was only 6.30 am. Had the excitement gotten to me? I gazed at the gable end wall for more than an hour as I tried to visualize the great man kicking the leather high and springing to catch it time and time again. Later I wandered down to Kingstown pier and in my mind's eye saw him row his boat across the bay on the night he captained Kerry to victory in the 1959 All-Ireland final. This journey was repeated on many summer nights after training with Kerry.

Having satisfied myself that I had absorbed enough to write a poem in his honour, I returned to my room and penned the following tribute to the still model of perfection in Gaelic Football
- my childhood hero Mick O Connell.

The Islandman

I stood alone on Kingstown pier
Enchanted by the view,
For since my youth I dreamed of here
And all because of you,
And I had longed to step ashore
Upon the hallowed ground,
Where you did train in days of yore
With diligence profound.

I took the road down to Glanleam
And sat for half a day,
Beside the house where you did dream
Of football games and play
The leather high with pride and joy
Against the gable wall,
And you a young barefooted boy
Did practise to enthral.

Oh it was good to revisit
That image in my mind,
For I found there the true spirit
That you had once entwined
With skill innate and steadfast faith
In football pure and true,
Why still today when men play great
They are compared with you.

Along the path down to the bay
I strolled through pasture green,
Here in your youth you saved the hay
With island men serene,
I watched the waves break off the rocks
The gulls swoop overhead,
And far away from men and clocks
I felt quite comforted.

'Tis well you steered a steady line
At night across the swell,
With thoughts of home you did align
Your little vessel well,
And if at times you were remote
We idolised you still,
"The Islandman," the purists wrote,
"Exudes with class and skill."

'Tis said the fuchsias cast their seeds
From Glanleam's garden fair,
No purer than your football deeds
When springing to the air,
And from the top of Yeokaun Hill
Quite stunning is the view,
But as I sat there in the chill
My thoughts were still with you.

For when God set this place apart
With beauty to behold,
He must have had within his heart
Love for the green and gold,
For just as seedlings need the rain
Valentia needed you,
In his wisdom God did ordain
A talent rare and true

THE BLOOMING OF THE GAEL

Give glory to our native games
That have sustained us o'er the years,
When pain and anguish dimmed the flames
Of liberty and hope with tears,
When our forefathers bravely stood
Together all for freedom's cause,
And played the games they understood
To spurn the cruel penal laws.

Give praise to those with vision who
Roused up the garsuns of the land,
Who thrilled on playing games anew
With talent great and spirit grand,
Who all around the countryside
Sprung forth to play for Ireland's cause,
And music too flowed with the tide
And dance and verse to great applause.

Give thanks to stars from every age
Who thrilled the crowds with flair and verve,
In games that filled a sporting page
With wonder words they did deserve,
And thanks to those who never played
The hallowed sod in Thurles town,
But loyal to the club they stayed
During times when spirits were down.

Give respect to fine men of chalk
For words of wisdom o'er the years,
For teaching boys to walk the walk
And catch a flying ball to cheers,
To those who followed on O' Hehir
On the airways with golden voice,
To those who took the pen and chair
At AGMs, for them rejoice.

Give honour to the referees
And our beloved Artane Band,
To all who served on committees
And women folk who lent a hand,
To those who travelled near and far
And cheered their team in a great clash,
The man who painted the crossbar
And the skilled one who cut the ash.

Give glory to our native games
That have sustained us o'er the years,
To those who modified the aims
To those who raised Croke Park's great tiers,
To those who carry on a way
Of life so good in Ireland free,
For Cusack and men of his day
Give thanks for peace and liberty.

THE JOY WAS HIS, THE JOY WAS MINE

Well I could not have been as glad
Had I pulled off that wonder save,
Than I was for my youngest lad
Who on the line stood tall and brave,
And threw himself against the post
To turn the ball a foot outside,
Oh it was heavenly almost
To see him thump the air with pride.

For a whole week he pranced about
The garden in his football strip,
It made me glad to hear him shout,
"He saves it with his finger tip,"
And friend and neighbour did applaud
That happy little boy of ten,
And confidence was his reward
When he took to the field again.

Now six feet four and eighteen years
No longer that small chubby boy,
But fit and lean, I felt the tears
Come to my eyes last night with joy,
A penalty, the final kick
He stood upright on the goal line,
A super save, a wonder flick
The joy was his, the joy was mine.

COWARD

I shan't forget that boy O'Dell
The shy lad in our class,
Picked to read the Epistle well
At the end of term mass.

Before the president and dean
Before the parents all,
The young boy hardly yet fourteen
Was up there to enthral.

Missal in hand he stood upright
And then began to talk,
But I noticed his legs go light
His face grow white as chalk.

The more he read the worse he shook
We thought that he would fall,
Thought I, I'll go and hold the book
And help him to stand tall.

But my mates laughed there in the pew
And I had not the nerve,
To help my friend faithful and true
The least he did deserve.

He mumbled through and in the seat
He sat there at my side,
I was the one to taste defeat
He was the one with pride.

FINGERS

When I was young I counted on
My fingers when in school,
For often they were called upon
To save me ridicule,
Behind my back I counted out
The sum of two and three,
And when I was in any doubt
My fingers rescued me.

Back in my prime I loved to spring
With vigour from the ground,
Oh it was such a great feeling
Opponents to astound,
With fingers taut I thought of nought
Except to win the ball,
And many's the kick out I caught
With pure joy I recall.

My poetry is simple lore
But still it brings me joy,
To rhyme a word with commodore
McIver, ship ahoy,
My fingers dip the pen in ink
Write words at sober pace,
The more I write the more I think
I'm blessed with luck and grace.

But spare a thought dear gentle friend
For those who write and draw
With nothing on which to depend
Except their mouth and jaw,
Let's pay them tribute and exalt
The wonder of their skill,
Their spirit is a treasure vault
Of talent to fulfill.

A Sporting Chance

So icy cold it was that night
When there inside the shed
I placed my little calf so light
Down on a thick straw bed,
I thought she would not see the morn'
For she was spent and weak,
A month before her time was born
And not even a squeak.

Thought I, she's earned a sporting chance
As I turned on the lamp
Above her head with vigilance
In that house cold and damp,
I propped her up with lots of straw
While putting in her mouth
A nipple so that I could draw
The life inside her out.

I was relieved to see her suck
The nipple in my hand,
And when she gave a little buck
I knew that she was grand,
I stayed with her until daybreak
Till she was snug and warm,
The small calf I could not forsake
That night in the snow storm.

That little calf is now a cow
The finest in the herd,
And each night when I wipe my brow
A song of joy is heard,
If I could wave a magic wand
A fighting chance I'd give,
To hungry child and vagabond
The gift of life to live.

BEYOND THE NORM

Beyond the flowers in the lea,
Beyond the morning dew,
Beyond the moonlight on the sea,
Beyond the mountain view,
Beyond the sunshine on the pine,
Beyond the break of day,
I found the music so divine
That I was swept away.

Beyond the ecstasy of love,
Beyond a waterfall,
Beyond the comfort of a glove,
Beyond the winning ball,
Beyond a sapphire or diamond,
Beyond a boat off shore,
The music took me way beyond
These pleasures and much more.

I was transfixed and for a while
Stood rooted to the ground,
That movement helped me reconcile
My soul with splendid sound,
And in a moment did transform
My thoughts on gifts so rare,
For this was way beyond the norm
And Schubert's heart was there.

What genius there is in a piece
That lasts the test of time,
And gives the listener release
In music, verse or rhyme,
That takes him gently to a place
He knows not why or where,
But in a moment can embrace
Feelings beyond compare.

UP AND AWAY

Oh pretty swallows let me praise
Your industry o'er recent days,
With diligence and pride and zest
You come and go into your nest,
And my company you ignore
For you have seen me heretofore,
Your cosy spot, no orchard tree
But in the cowshed here with me.

Oh pretty swallows on the gate
How well you both co-operate,
And guard your nest with eagle eye
From the concerns of the magpie,
I see you soaring through the air
With gaiety I do declare,
Rest up a while for in a day
You will have three small chicks, I pray.

Oh pretty swallows in and out
How busy you are hereabout,
For your brood it is supper time
The frenzy of their bills, sublime,
You come and go at frantic pace
Then dive like lightning out of space,
And Oh how happy is your note
Each time you feed a hungry throat.

Oh pretty swallows take a bow
Your fledglings are well nurtured now,
Up on a ledge I see them perch
Soon they will sing high on a church,
And now they flutter round the shed
Excited and good spirited,
Ho-Ho I see them through the door
Up and away for evermore.

Phonecall after Dark

She lights the lamp upon the windowsill
And for a while she gazes at its glow,
Outside the wind is blowing cold and shrill
The mountainside is dusted up with snow.

The silken sheen ensnares her in a trance
The snowflakes brush against the windowpane,
Her mind is racing round like in a dance
And pondering she surveys the terrain.

The rising smoke brings comfort to her now
She gazes at the house not far away,
In the distance she hears a mooing cow
And thinks about past summers, making hay.

It's lonesome here for she is all alone
Like a boatman sailing throughout the night,
She thinks she hears the ringing telephone
But silence greets her answer of delight.

And now she prays "Hail Mary full of grace…"
Her brittle fingers move along the beads,
There is holiness etched upon her face
"Forgive us all our trespasses…" she pleads.

Her whispered words portray a great desire
To be profound in her discourse with God,
She's cosy now beside the kitchen fire
And in a little while begins to nod.

And now she wakes and calls a name out loud
But he has long since left and doesn't hear,
She takes his picture down and is so proud
To see her lovely boy from yesteryear.

Her youngest son with golden curls so fair
Takes her on a jaunt of complete delight,
She sees him swinging gently through the air
She hears him calling gaily in the night.

Ah memories hold her fast in a spell
She smiles and knows they make her glad for now,
Her yearnings like a bucket in a well
That goes as deep as the rope will allow.

Now old and grey her heart is beating fast
She sees her house the focal point of fun,
But that she knows is in the distant past
Now she hopes for an audience of one.

A single soul to help her pass the day
Or maybe share her stories after dark,
A friend to call when passing on his way
To cheer her up just like the thrush or lark.

She dims the lamp upon the windowsill
And once again she gazes round the room,
The snow is falling thickly now and still
She waits for a phone call to lift the gloom.

It's lonesome here for she is all alone

By The Seashore

One sparkling day of summer time
I found a parkside bench,
And settled with my book of rhyme
My thirst for calm to quench,
Oh it was well away from view
And facing the seashore,
The perfect place to find anew
Some inner peace and more.

But down beside me sat a chap
And with him two young boys,
With his head bowed down to his lap
Those two made lots of noise,
Around the seat they danced high jinks
(They were but four or five),
They threw sweet paper, squirted drinks
And to the ground did dive.

You know how you can overlook
Bad manners for peace sake,
But when I could not read my book
Exception I did take,
"Excuse me Sir," said I polite
(He seemed so far away),
"But your two kids are cross, a mite
Could you calm them I pray?"

"I'm sorry Sir" he meekly said
The shortcoming is mine,
He murmured as he raised his head
"They normally are fine,"
Said he with sad and tearful eyes
"I don't know what to say
To my two happy little boys,
Their mum has passed away."

MAMMA'S LETTERS

Dear Mamma, how I used to love
The letters that you sent each week,
They were a blessing from above
And used to rouse me so to speak,
Away back when I was a boy
Away at school and on my own,
Your letters brought me so much joy
That seeds of confidence were sown.

Oh I remember clearly still
Familiar words that did delight,
And sometimes on the window sill
And sometimes in my bed at night
I read the loving words you wrote
About my friends and you and Dad,
And often you enclosed a note
Perhaps the last one that you had.

My lines to you were all about
A goal I scored, a game I won,
And looking back without a doubt
You thought I was a super son,
It gladdened me to make you proud
When I passed well a written test
That put you floating on a cloud,
And then I knew that I was blessed.

Oh how I wish that I had kept
Those letters that you sent to me,
For nowadays I must accept
Such writing is a rarity,
But back when north winds whispered low
And I was tucked up in my bed,
I kept there beneath my pillow
Your loving letters I had read.

THE PENALTY

Sure I was in the dressing room the day all hell broke lose
When Jack Dawley's pep- up talk prompted torrents of abuse,
The game was late because our team was delayed going out
And our participation was for certain in some doubt.
It all started the week before in our last practice match
When we won a penalty kick we thought we would dispatch,
Ger Batt Murphy took the ball and he placed it on the spot
But nearly hit the corner flag instead of the jackpot.

Well this was just a practice match so there was no crisis
Not a word was said to Ger Batt about his awful miss,
Till we gathered one week later for the last game of the year
The final of the Junior B and Jack Dawley made it clear.
That everyone that ever came from our neck of the woods
When playing in a final always came up with the goods,
This was the kind of pressure talk we could have done without
But still we knew if we played well we were in with a shout.

Jack stood inside the dressing room and gave a rousing speech
And started with the goalie and great focus did beseech,
And on he went down through the team and spoke to every man
You know the way that coaches do roaring pure inhuman.
Well to be fair we listened well for we all knew our job
From taking frees and sideline kicks to watching for a lob,
And we were ready for the fight and breaking down the door
When Jack Dawley lowered his voice like he'd not done before.

Said he, "Now, boys, before you go there's one last thing to say
In case the opposition get a penalty today,
Let Ger Batt Murphy take it 'cause between Ballyheen Piers
He wouldn't score a penalty," and we laughed out in tears.
Well Ger Batt was the wicked sort and made for Dawley's throat
The Murphys and the Dawleys used language I cannot quote,
By the time we reached the field our team was in disarray
And lost the Novice final by fourteen points on that day.

(Ballyheen Piers near Kanturk Co.Cork are 6m high and 80m apart)

THE DAY I BEAT MICK HOGAN
FOR A TANNER

At half past nine the day was fine, said Mick Hogan to me,
"Let's play a game and I will shame you twenty one to three,
The alley's clear, there's no one near, bring on your windy ball
We'll have a bet, lest you forget, to keep it on the wall."
So off we went with great intent to play a handball game
A tanner down for the showdown we practised with our aim,
Mick tossed an ace and on his face I saw a crafty smile
Oh Gosh! Thought I, I'll have to try and play with better style.

The game was close for I suppose the two of us were even
We played each day for fun and play in alley, pitch and garden,
But not for cash and so this clash was in another sphere
With sixpence down for the showdown great tension did appear.
At nineteen- all Mick hit the ball high into the canal
I yelled and roared as the ball soared, no way to treat a pal,
For half an hour till he got sour we searched without success
But 'twas my toss and I was cross with Michael's childishness.

A new ball bought, no more we fought though I was down nine
pence
Now one ace clear with triumph near I tossed with confidence,
With temper fraught Mick thought of naught except lose the
new ball
He hit it high into the sky a mile above the wall,

Now on his back I pulled him back as he made for the door
He said, "You're mad," I said, "You're sad," and felled him to the floor,
Then to the shop I had to pop to buy another ball
I tossed the ace, to see his face was worth the cash and brawl.

But though I won it was no fun to pay my one and six
'Twas a dear game but all the same I beat him at his tricks,
We soon made up, he made a cup, and we went to the field
Where he was Ring and was dazzling his new rig out revealed,
From gap to gap without mishap we played an hour or more,
I think he won and said, "Well done," we lost track of the score,
Then off we went and were content to take our comics out,
He was a friend that was Godsend; thank God he's still about!

MISTER BEAN

Now Mister Bean invited me
Come and review my policy,
At rates attractive on the day
For just a fraction of my pay,
Said he, "It makes good sense for sure
To invest more to be secure,
When you retire at sixty-five
This pension will help you to thrive."

A perky chap was Mister Bean
You know the type, well dressed and lean,
Designer glasses on his nose
On his lapel a fragrant rose,
And on his desk a laptop grand
With figures everywhere at hand,
He spoke with a most reserved tone
When answering his mobile phone.

Said he, "Come here look at this graph
In the last year went up by half,
The stocks and shares are very good
Oil's coming down the way it should,
The building's great, we're in a boom
I have no doubt it will mushroom,
And that is why you should invest
And reap a bountiful harvest."

Well I signed up and so would you
Went off and bought a car brand new,
And kindly friends who sought advice
I told invest not once but twice,
Said I, "I have it from a mate
For twenty years all will be great,
He works with figures sharp and keen
My friend the lovely Mister Bean."

Then came the crash, a somersault
The building grinded to a halt,
The graph that was on upward trail
Now turned around and grew a tail,
The oil went up, the shares came down
And Mister Bean moved out of town,
I rang his office just today
The nice girl said, "He's gone away."

So now my shares have no value
And I am short of revenue,
The nest egg that would make me bloom
Has now a projection of doom,
Ten years to go to sixty-five
The day he said that I would thrive,
Life is ok but funds are lean
Oh where, oh where is Mister Bean?

ODE TO A SPOON

Oh wooden spoon I swore the day
You came into my life to stay,
In the top drawer with spoon and knife
You were the bane of my young life,
You were called on in time of need
And often chased me at high speed,
You stalked me out in hut and shed
And oftentimes beneath my bed.

Oh wooden spoon I ran a mile
Every time you turned on the style,
Round kitchen table, chair and stool
I ducked each time that you did rule
With smacks chastising to my butt
As I slammed the kitchen door shut,
You were the one I feared the most
I knew my rear end you could roast.

Oh wooden spoon how flexible
You were when I was horrible
And up to tricks and devilment,
'Twas you dished out the punishment,
One moment mixing batter up
The next chasing me like a pup,
'Twas you decided right from wrong
When I was getting wild and strong.

Oh wooden spoon have you been here
In this old trunk year after year?
I must have put you out of sight
To save my butt some frosty night,
I bear no grudge you did your job
We were no saints myself and Bob,
I am happy now to call it quits
Those bygone days I love to bits.

REPOSE

Back when I burned the midnight oil
I lacked desire for mirth,
And often weary was my toil
More grief than it was worth,
I struggled vainly for a plot
To write a little ode,
The more I tried the worse it got
For heavy was my load.

But later on I met a man
And wise and bold was he,
Said he, "Young boy devise a plan
Then rest and let it be,
Let it ferment and instinctive
Your thoughts in rhyme will flow,
Your words will be so descriptive
You'll write pure as the snow."

So now when jumbled are my words
I set my pencil down,
And go and walk amongst the birds
Or don my dressing gown,
Then when I rise up with the lark
My words flow clear I find,
For just as a fire needs a spark
Sleep stimulates the mind.

GOLDEN CURLS

I sat upon the barber's chair
My unkempt hair to cut,
And quickly I became aware
Of grey hair at my foot,
And if the truth be told mayhap
A tinge of white upon my lap.

The little boy there at my side
Sat on his mother's knee,
Oh he was handsome and bright-eyed
As bonny as can be,
And golden were the curls that fell
Upon the lap where he did yell.

He cried a thousand tiny tears
Each time the lady went
To cut the curls around his ears
'Till she was nearly spent,
She gave him sweets and lollipops
And promises of toys from shops.

Then as I looked down on the floor
At gold amongst the grey,
I hankered for my youth once more
That long had passed away,
And I'd have shed those thousand tears
If I could have rolled back the years.

Now safely back down on the floor
Once more he was polite,
And as he went out through the door
With Mom he did unite,
I blessed that boy with golden curls
As his long path in life unfurls.

DANGEROUS LIAISONS

I saw them kissing down our street
With passion and desire,
That morning both of them did meet
Like kids with hearts on fire,
Then to the country they did go
Where he told her he loved her so.

When they returned with feelings high
There on the street once more
She kissed her bloke to say goodbye
With passion like before,
While I could only watch and smile
And see them walking down the aisle.

That night she whispered to a friend
"Surely he'll leave his wife,
I know on him I can depend
For a romantic life,
To Paris maybe or to Rome
We'll go and build a happy home."

And to our street - a year perhaps
To meet they came each week,
It was like turning on the taps
Of passion so to speak,
I'd never seen such fun before
Right there outside the village store.

Not young ones these with sporty dress
They were as old as me,
And on the street with eagerness
They were bold as can be,
Miss Murphy turned the other way
When they smooched outside her doorway.

Not nosey I but in our place
There's not much to observe,
And when two lovers here embrace
You think oh what a nerve!
From fifty miles they came to meet
And never once were they discreet.

But just as summer passes by
So did their love grow dim,
One day she looked him in the eye
She had grown tired of him,
For though each week he brought a rose
His wife still had him I suppose.

And so our street is empty now
(Miss Murphy won't complain),
That evening they had a bad row
Her efforts were in vain,
Tearful she whispered to her friend
"His behaviour I can't defend."

A juicy story you'll agree
But have I got it wrong?
Maybe the two of them were free
For romance pure all along,
Make up your mind Paris or Rome
Or is he with his wife at home?

The Donkey Derby

'Twas for the donkey derby at the carnival in Glin
Ned Dawley said he'd take his chance and put his donkey in,
No finer mule was there around than Dawley's well fed ass
For horse and cart and dog and hound at great speed he could
pass,
A week before the festival Ned Dawley said to me,
"Come here to me, young fellow, and sit up on my donkey,"
Well up I went and off he took at a ferocious pace
"Well by golly," said Ned Dawley, "we're goin' to win the race."

I practised every day that week though I was feeling sore
With blisters on my backside which were quite hard to ignore,
But we became acquainted soon the fine young ass and me
"We'll make the running from the start," that was Ned's strategy,
And so it was the night before the race down in the pub
Ned got a lotion from a pal to give the ass a rub,
"There's nothing left to chance," said he, "I will be leading in
The winner of the derby at the carnival in Glin.

Then there was great debate over what Ned would call the ass
Someone said "Dawley's Flyer" since the animal had class,
But he settled on "Banjo" and I was over the moon
When they dressed me in breeches with a jacket of maroon,
You'd think it was the Curragh we were going to next day
For half the village folk came out to see us on our way,
And Ned Dawley was twisted from a dozen pints of stout
They had to help him down in Glin to lead the donkey out.

Well talk of complications as we headed to the start
I saw there was a fence to jump and nearly fell apart,
It wasn't in our master plan to jump a bale of straw
And with me up on Banjo it was too late to withdraw,
Ned Dawley staggered over as we lined up at the rope
His intentions were as slippery as a bar of soap,
He slipped a device to me and said, "Put it in your pocket
Before the fence give him a jab, he'll take off like a rocket."

Now the starter had a whisker that stretched down to his knees
Before him stood ten donkeys of various pedigrees,
Said he, "You know the rule, young boys, 'tis first man past the post
And by the carnival marquee the winner we will toast."
The flag went down and I shot off and straight into the lead
And Banjo was eating up ground with his usual speed,
A quarter mile beyond the bend the winning post I saw
But first we had to jump over the bloody bale of straw.

I heard Ned Dawley calling out, "Time now to give the prod"
The electric shock I took out, jabbed Banjo with the rod,
Well he stopped up and I was thrown a mile above the fence
And Banjo turned and ran back down to where we did commence,
The trickster with the whisker was jumping around with glee
And so were half a dozen who were on the committee,
Ned Dawley said it was a fix to have the bale to jump
I went home with egg on my face and a gigantic lump.

THE YANK

I was at school that summer's day, the day The Yank sat down,
And we took to him straightaway with his mischievous frown,
We gathered round him like gadflies gather around a cow,
Said he, "I'm pleased to meet you guys, go easy on me now."
His accent like a singing bird was music to the ear,
And if we never said a word he'd chatter for a year,
Said he, "In the United States why everything is swank"
He so impressed me and my mates we christened him The Yank.

For weeks to come we sat in class together side by side,
And I would lend him my compass and he'd lend me his slide,
He'd prompt me with a Latin verb when I stood up all dumb,
At English prose he was superb and scored the maximum.
But all the same we dosed a bit at the back of the room,
And more than once I do admit we were given the broom
To brush the corridor or hall, for punishment 'twas said,
But we'd go playing basketball out in the court instead.

It was in the basketball court The Yank exuded class,
And I played with him for support just to provide the pass,
He'd find the net from out the line with a shot overhead,
And for him I'd be on cloud nine when he would knock 'em dead.
Then when the school team played in Cork they'd call out "watch
The Yank,"

They knew that he was from New York with every shot he sank,
With arms outstretched boys gathered round to shield him from
the ball,
But when the net once more was found "like Willis Reed"
he'd call.

His fuse was short and on the court it was his one drawback,
When teams went out to spoil the sport courage he did not lack,
But on the bench he was a loss, we could not ride the storm,
When he was out we lacked the gloss and courage to perform.
But beans and chips would compensate on days we felt defeat,
Down Patrick Street me and my mate would find a place to eat,
When funds were scarce we added up the coins there in my hand,
We often drank from the same cup with speed to beat the band.

The months passed by, one day he said, "I'm leaving at years
end,"
That night I lay awake in bed while thinking of my friend,
Said he, "Next fall when you visit I'll show you sights so rare
With designs that are exquisite and rich beyond compare.
I'll take you up the Empire State, bigger than half of Cork,
Then we will go and roller-skate our way throughout New York,
We'll take a ride to Gaelic Park where all your heroes played,
And late at night up in the dark you'll see great lights displayed."

The school was in holiday mood the day the movie came,
We looked forward with gratitude to seeing stars of fame,
With chairs laid out there was a shout, a banging of the door,
But no one was seen there about except glass on the floor.
Along the wall stood one and all but no one took the blame,
"Who broke the door with the football?" asked the Dean in a flame,
The silence there was such I swear you'd hear a small pin drop,
And he was cross beyond compare and went and closed the shop.

We sat inside the study hall with great cause for regret,
The fellow who had kicked the ball had not admitted yet,
We wouldn't see the movie now or our hero John Wayne,
And all because there was a row over who broke the pane.
Just then the Prefect rang the bell; we were called to the hall,
Who broke the glass no one could tell and no one found the ball,
A whisper went round that The Yank admitted to the crime,
We saw the film, I drew a blank and left before the time.

Alone he sat disconsolate inside the study hall,
The movie was the ultimate, everyone had a ball,
All of next day while we did play The Yank was kept inside,
And then he left on holiday, and all that night I cried.
He did not come back the next year and I had lost a chum,
"There is a diff'rent atmosphere," I wrote home to my mum,
When I think back on that great crash I can say honestly,
That when I heard the windows smash The Yank was sat with me.

SNOW WHITE

One day inside a city tram
I sat beside a child,
Oh he was quiet as a lamb
And with politeness smiled,
How good it is to see, thought I,
A gracious young boy filled with joy.

The tram was packed along the aisle
Commuters everyone,
All creeds all classes to beguile
And each one on the run,
Some smiling faces to behold
Some weary like and wan and old.

A dwarf stepped on close to our seat
We saw him through the door,
And he looked aged and dead beat
While standing on the floor,
He barely reached a grown man's waist
My little friend got up in haste.

"Excuse me, Sir," said he with grace,
"But you can have my seat,
It's pretty crowded round this place
Soon I'll be on the street,"
I shan't forget the dwarf's reply
"Do not insult me, silly boy."

I was dumbfounded by his stance
The little child sat down,
And was afraid to even glance
Up before the next town,
'Twas a put down he could not take
Even one smile he could not fake.

At the next stop across the way
A lady stood to leave,
Before she went to the doorway
She caught him by the sleeve,
"Your Mam would be so proud," said she,
"You were as noble as can be."

Then to the dwarf she simply said,
"Snow White would not be pleased,"
It was clear that she was well-read
The young boy's pain was eased,
A princely deed turned out to be
A lesson in propriety.

Preview to next Poem

"For there's something in a Sunday that makes a body feel alone."

Kris Kristofferson - "Sunday Morning Coming Down."

When I listen to Kris Kristofferson singing "Sunday Morning Coming Down," I always think of an old man I spoke to in my village many years ago. He had worked in London for some years. I had just returned from a a short vacation in London when I said to him that I was taken with the excitement and the buzz and it would be very easy to settle in London. "young man," he said, "London can be one of the loneliest places in the world on a Sunday afternoon." For many people, Sunday can be different to other days and I certainly can identify with the writer in this song.

I penned this tribute to the great man and gave him a framed copy during his tour in Ireland in 2010.On receiving it he gave me a signed picture saying, "Thanks for the Poetry Phillip", which I shall always treasure. Kris Kristofferson remains one of the truly great songwriters of our time.

For Kris Kristofferson

You help us make it through the night
When we are ill at ease,
For like a little bird in flight
Your words float through the breeze
And soothe us when we need repose
And lift us in the morn',
For pure they are just like a rose,
Golden like sheaves of corn.

With Sunday morning coming down
When we have lost our way,
And put up in some lonesome town
We cannot face the day,
Your words and music give us hope
To fight the devil there,
Somehow we find the strength to cope
Lay our transgressions bare.

But most of all it's on the stage
We see the hand of God
In you, an icon of an age,
And think like when he trod
On water 'twas a miracle-
And so it is with you,
Your music is the pinnacle
Of life, so great and true.

THE SNAPSHOOTER

She crossed the covered bridge each day
But never stopped to look
At the great beauty on display,
Like ripples in a brook.

Until he came and with his lens
He took it for his own,
Used it his consciousness to cleanse
His intellect to hone.

A snapshot of a place in time
He hung up at her place,
He didn't ask her for a dime
But kissed her in embrace.

She saw the bridge for what it was,
Knew now that it was fair,
She sat and looked at it because
She knew he had been there.

It is the image of his face
She sees upon the wall,
The kiss that time will not erase
The stranger lean and tall.

THIS TOO WILL PASS

Old pal your head is bent and low
There's weight upon your back,
You look so weary as you go
The clouds above are black,
You dread tomorrow and you stare
Into the looking glass,
Try your best to become aware
Old pal this too will pass.

You lack the will to climb the hill
You have no wish to smile,
You're feeling gloomy in the chill
Yet you can't walk a mile,
You feel alone, stuck to the spot
The dullest in the class,
The storm passes on, does it not?
Old pal this too will pass.

Observe the mood like you can watch
Yourself across a room,
Then see it absorbed like a splotch
Being cleansed by a broom,
Then watch the darkness turn to light
Like snowflakes at Christmas,
For sure as summer days are bright
Old pal this too will pass.

THE JOY OF GIVING

By thy infinite power Lord
Grant that there might be
Due conformity and accord
In our love for thee.

And grant that we might see thy face
In our fellow man,
That we might welcome and embrace
Your words and your plan.

Help us be easy with ourselves,
To accept due blame,
That we might leave upon the shelves
Our faults in thy name.

And as we journey on life's way
Help us understand
The beauty of the night and day
Has come from thy hand.

So that we might appreciate
The joy of living,
For thy sake let us celebrate
The joy of giving.

A Different Kind of Sunday

'Twas the final, I had to play,
Just could not leave my comrades down,
My spirit was in disarray
My whole world had come tumbling down.

The game was on, the play intense,
My opponent got in to score,
He was a star at my expense
And I should have been called ashore.

But I played on and did my best
Not for myself but for the team,
On days like this the acid test
Is hanging on when out of steam.

But clearly I did not prevail
Like I had done the year before,
My rival left me in his trail
And put his teammates to the fore.

I shook his hand, softly crying,
The game was furthest from my mind,
My dear Mam in bed lay dying
And answers I just could not find.

A LITTLE NONSENSE

A little nonsense now and then
Is cherished by the wisest men.

Let's sing a song to nonsense and
To twaddle of all sort,
To balderdash to beat the band,
To blather long and short,
To poppycock for sport.

Let's sing a song to those who play
The prankster to amuse,
And brighten up the darkest day
With laughter to enthuse,
And antics to confuse.

Let's sing to him who takes the stage
And sings a hearty song
With fire and gusto to engage
His friends the whole night long,
And revel in the throng.

Let's sing to those who costumes wear
For fun at Halloween,
Who dress up as a Teddy Bear,
A king or Beauty Queen,
Or an Irish Colleen.

Let's sing to those who take a pen
To lighten up the mood,
To circus clown, comedienne,
Those with fun attitude,
We owe our gratitude.

For what is life without some fun,
Great knowledge without joy,
A little nonsense in the sun
Makes Jack a brighter boy,
Worth gold as life goes by.

WHO SAID THAT BEAUTY FADES?

It must have been a summer's day
With flowers in full bloom,
For she looked stunning in that way
When she stepped in the room,
And all the boys out in the yard
Agreed that she was class,
The new teacher set a standard
That no one could surpass.

It must have been an English test
For which I got a star,
For I told mom that I was best
At poetry by far,
And though I was but eight years old
I think I fell in love,
With my teacher who to behold
Was sent from God above.

For when I wrote above the line
With one eye covered over,
She told me I was doing fine
And admired my pullover,
And bit by bit that lazy eye
Grew sharper than a blade,
She gave me sweets, said not to cry
When daft mistakes were made.

Last week I met her in the street
Still filled with charm and grace,
And oh what joy it was to meet,
Old footsteps to retrace,
A half a century's passed by
She still retains her beauty,
This teacher who did edify
During the course of duty.

It brought me back to happy days
To rumble, tumble sound,
To pageants and to small school plays
And music to astound,
And as I journeyed through the night
She won my accolades,
Thought I there's nothing black and white
Who said that beauty fades?

SANDY

The fire is glowing nicely and I'm settled for the night
Oh how I love the comfort of my home,
The snow is falling gently and the ground outside is white
I'm flicking through the pages of my tome,
The silence here is golden and with scholarly intent
I'm reading about places far away,
The truth is when the ship sailed out I marked myself absent
This is my home and I am here to stay.

I ventured out but yesterday and stood and gazed around
At the valley all carpeted with snow,
It was a joy to meditate while I absorbed the sound
Of the stream swelling in the glen below,
I could have been just any place on earth on that fair morn,
And not the sense of beauty would I find
To compare with that peaceful spot close to where I was born
And have lived with my neighbours good and kind.

For eighty years and seven I have passed along this way
Since I was a young girl going to school,
I have seen snowdrops in springtime and kissed the summer
spray
And felt the autumn evenings turning cool,
For all the lure of nature and the beauty unrefined
The evenings I spent dreaming on a log,
I long to go back to my house where my life is defined
By my kitchen, my garden and my dog.

Ah Sandy is my little dog the one who lives with me
In my small dwelling on the village street,
Of all the doggies in the world to have for company
There's none with that young puppy could compete,
She greets me every morning with her paws upon my lap
Her youthful face excited filled with fun,
And sometimes in the evening when I take a little nap
She snuggles up beside me in the sun.

I'm smiling as I watch her sitting on the garden seat
Puzzled it seems while staring at a thrush,
While up above in safety the air is filled with tweet
And I am captivated by the bush,
Then off she scampers hastily like a kid in the yard
She's fuelled with high spirits passing by,
And I am left there watching with the greatest of regard
For my doggie, the birdies and the sky.

She's always close beside me while I am doing my chores
Hanging on to my coat tails all day through,
Whenever I am baking she is waiting on all fours
And dives down for a biscuit like a smew,
And whisper here I talk to her in tones she understands
She wags her tail excited and alive,
Then nuzzles her small head against my old and wrinkled hands
Sure in her company I seem to thrive.

But most of all in winter nights when I am all alone
And mellow is the music that I hear,
When sometimes drowsy by the fire I think of folk I've known
And in the twighlight hour might shed a tear,
She's constantly beside me to bring comfort in distress
Her ears pricked up she looks with loving eyes,
At the foot of my bed she nestles like a shepherdess
The flurry in my brain she pacifies.

We're both here in my cosy house beside the firelight glow
And to the world outside we scarcely rate,
But now I hail you faithful dog tonight and tomorrow
You are my sole companion and my mate,
You are the one who makes me feel secure on winter nights
The reason I go out on summer days,
You are the joy inside my home the source of my delights
God Bless you Sandy for your cheerful ways.

THE COMPLEXITIES OF LIFE

He's standing at the counter where he rests up every night,
The banker who spends half his pay is reserved and polite,
He's staring at the bottles with his customary stare,
With the silence of a man who is playing solitaire.
And if there is ought on his mind he shields it with his life,
Though it is said no divan bed does he share with his wife,
And every night from eight till late he downs dry gin or scotch,
While staring at the bright labels and ignoring his watch.

See Rodney Ellis at the bar a master of the art
Of chatting up young ladies who are elegant and smart,
Then to his pad he takes them for beverages and for fun,
They scale the heights of Everest and then he's on the run.
Here nightly he brags all about the conquests he has made,
While eyeing up another lass to ply his sorry trade,
In a damp room a child cries out - a babe without her dad,
Rodney Ellis is not about nor does he think it sad.

From 'cross the river comes George Jones who's all beat up and
lame
And wounded with a broken heart got in the dating game,
Each night he tells the sorry tale about finding in bed
His sweetheart with a dentist chap - soon they were to be wed.
Dishevelled is his hair and clothes his comforts they are few,
Though nightly he drinks seven pints sitting on the same pew,
She robbed him of his happiness - he's robbed himself of joy,
A pity that he'll never hold a bouncing baby boy.

There is great welcome in the bar when Tom steps in for one,
He's old and grey, has had his day working in midday sun,
For fifty years of wedded bliss he's loved his Mary well,
Tonight he left her with a kiss, she holds him in her spell.
Beside the banker at the bar he sips his pint of stout,
Respectful of the way things are he doesn't seek him out,
In an hour's time he'll climb the stairs with Mary on his arm,
The two of them a happy pair are filled with grace and charm.

He makes his point with arrogance, the argument is o'er,
And lesser mortals yield to him down on the barroom floor,
Joe Mango sees it as his right to correct right from wrong,
And kindly folk with concepts clear are fed up with his song.
With elbows on the counter and a pint of ale to booth,
His story is monotonous and not always the truth,
At home his supper's ready and though it's past time for bed
His anxious wife waits up for him with patience and with dread.

She's wearing an engagement ring her romance is complete,
Samantha and her handsome beau have stepped in from the
street,
Up at the bar they take a stool and soon the cocktails flow,
But if they are excited then the others do not show.
With tenderness he takes her hand, looks in her hazel eyes,
They talk about a wedding band, another drink he buys,
There is desire and there is love, if promises are true,
Soon she will live in a fine house with a long avenue.

The banker calls for one last scotch before "last orders please"
Rodney Ellis looks at his watch, is off for a Chinese,
Joe Mango listens to George Jones; they should listen to Tom,
Samantha and her lover leave with laughter and aplomb.
These are the folk, who call each night to Hotel De Lorraine,
Who sit and think, enjoy a drink or nullify the pain
Of sins less cured and long endured, the struggle and the strife
The thoughts that stay won't go away, the complexities of life.

SERVICE WITH A SMILE

Oh Fox and Hounds its here I sit
And have been now for quite a bit,
A look of boredom on my face
Examining the empty place,
Close up the bar and go to bed
Or wait till someone calls instead,
Someone will call, they always do
Stay if they can till one or two,
Talking bunkum, I am all ears
And have been now for forty years,
Seen good times come and good times go
With no one else to run the show,
Oh Fox and Hounds I owe you nought
Though many lessons you have taught.

Its ten past ten Bold Sam arrives
I'm well used to his twists and jives,
"'Tis quiet tonight"-"'Tis that Sam"
(Tell him that I don't give a damn),
But hark there is the protocol
When I am serving alcohol,
Sit on the stool, open my ears
Prepare to go back fifty years,
Then listen well and be polite
Did Sam pay for his drink tonight?
Said Sam, "The good days are well gone"
I struggle to suppress a yawn,

"The young guard bagged two more" said he
"I always knew he was shifty."

My brain is dull. Is this burnout?
Sam wants another pint of stout,
"'Tis quiet alright"-"'Tis that Sam"
But now he's joined by Abraham,
They haven't spoken for ten years
Not my business, just fill the beers,
Talk nice to one, then the other
Treat each like he is a brother,
"'Tis soft tonight"-"'Tis Abraham"
(Tell him that I don't give a damn),
But no he's twelve months on the dole
Far better listen and console,
"The ministers have all the perks
That's right" said he "a pack of jerks."

Then silence save the radio
My repertoire is getting low,
Then Sam gives Abraham a dig
Something about his fathers pig,
I call out loud "Last orders please"
I check the gas, pretend to sneeze,
But Abraham is getting deaf
And didn't hear the word with F..,
Around and round my story goes
About a farmer and the crows,
I'm goin' brain dead, time to get out

Sam wants another pint of stout,
Abraham's heading for the door
Gives me a wink, I know the score.

It's ten past twelve, I'm back to one
A half an hour, my day is done,
Sam puts the glass up to his lips
It seems an hour before he sips,
Once more he drawls about the pig
"No harm to give your man a dig,"
Its closing time, I stay polite
Said I to Sam "We'll say goodnight,"
"Give me a drop and then I'm gone"
Said he and I let out a yawn,
I get the drop and then a dash
He gives me about half the cash,
The bar is up, solace is bought
Oh Fox and Hounds I owe you nought.

Mother Carroll

A Wonderful Irish Mother

When I was just a little lad
I met her in the village,
And a pleasant nature she had
When buying heads of cabbage,
Or bacon for her ten young boys
And three fine girls all growing,
Thought I, she is full of the joys
Of life with love bestowing.

A mother's love they used to know
Those children all so friendly,
For they grew up in her shadow
In her cottage so homely,
'Twas here they heard their father play
The mouth organ enchanting,
While mother put buns upon a tray
With homemade jam for spreading.

On Mondays with the washboard out
Ten times she boiled the kettle,
And scrubbed the clothes with fingers stout
With one eye on the cradle,
On the clothesline and fence and bush
She hung shirts and pullovers,
Then back to the kitchen she'd rush
To wash sheets and bed covers.

The boys did well and up in school
Each one helped out the other,
For Jack did share his book and rule
With Danny his young brother,
While mother in a field of beet
Was at a real tough station,
There in his pram her baby sweet
Slept under observation.

There was great fun inside the room
Of Bill and Con and Paddy,
But never a moment of gloom
While they shared bed with Christy,
Two up two down the coldest night
Saw them all snug and cosy,
When mother came to dim the light
She found them safe and dozy.

Georgie was so dear to her mum
She was her eldest daughter,
Regular as a pendulum
She left to cross the water,
And in the parcels that she sent
Were treats from London City,
For Sheila and Bernie content
To dress their dollies pretty.

Santa always brought a nice toy
To Tom and Noel and Gerry,
And each of them would jump with joy
Beneath the holly berry,
On Christmas night it was a sight
To see young Gordon singing,
And if she had to stop a fight
Mom would dish out the pudding.

On Sundays on his way to mass
Her friend Bill would be calling,
And sometimes they would share a glass
And stories so enthralling,
Bill saw each boy grow to a man
Well mannered and respectful,
And he knew where it all began;
With their mother so cheerful.

Many a man passed by her gate
And saw her there conversing
With Phillie her neighbour and mate,
Now she was older growing,
Her grandchildren all called around
With moms and dads so jolly,
And each time they were homeward bound
She gave each one a lolly.

The evening she was laid to rest
They stood together manful,
Her ten boys who to her were best
Her three girls who were tearful,
And as we shook them by the hand
We knew that Irish mother
Was dignified and warm and grand,
Had loved them like no other.

NELLIE

The girl next door was pretty and
I dearly wished that I
Could take her daily by the hand
Beneath the summer sky,
But other fellows wished that too
Which left me with no chance
To walk her 'neath the sky so blue
Or to the village dance.

But still I dreamed that one day soon
She would return my smile,
And out beneath a coral moon
We'd sit and talk awhile,
I'd look into her hazel eyes
And surely steal a kiss,
And warn her that the other boys
She really should dismiss.

Alas! My dreams did not come true
For she sailed o'er the sea,
And broken hearts she left a few
And one of them was me,
Upon the bridge we sat and yearned
For Nellie pure and sweet,
But sadly she never returned
To that house in our street.

Compo

When Ned Dawley fell down the hole
There was great consternation,
And he was resigned to the dole
During recuperation,
With money tight, thought he one night
"I will seek legal counsel,"
He met a lawyer young and bright
And told her what was gospel.

The plaintiff had his day in court
And came away elated,
"This man did not come here for sport,"
The ageing judge there stated,
"I award him five hundred pounds,
See how he is disabled,
The manhole in the council grounds
Should be covered or labelled."

Next week a bill came through his door
Three hundred pounds demanding,
Its contents shocked him to the core
These legal fees outstanding,
He made a beeline for the desk
Of Miss Belinda Ruddy,
Said he, "These charges are grotesque,
I thought you were my buddy."

Miss Ruddy swivelled in her chair
The matter contemplated,
Said she, "My legal fees are fair
They have not been inflated,
Two ninety five will clear your name
Please cut out the rigmarole,"
Said Ned Dawley, "Is this a game?
Which of us fell down the hole?"

GOD'S ANGELS

I wish I could forever be
The guardian of little birds,
Who flit and fly impressively
And summon up a host of words,
Who are the keepers of the sky
With twists and frolics to enjoy.

I wish I could forever hear
Their chorus exhilarating,
From trees and hedgerows far and near
Their melody is absorbing,
And when I see them in the morn'
I thank the Lord that I was born.

I wish that I could be as pure
As these the loveliest of things,
They are God's angels to be sure
His messengers of hope on wings,
And when I sit and watch them glide
I get a sense of calm inside.

I wish that I could be so true
As little birds are on the wing,
Their liveliness I love to view
Their modesty is uplifting,
And when I hear their evensongm
I know with them I do belong.

Pro-Am

I pitied the poor golfing chap
Whose drive went all askew,
He didn't even get a clap
But gales of laughter drew,
Down the fairway he meant to go
Drove at the crowd instead,
With face red as a tomato
He was devastated.

For six long months he'd waited for
This moment to arrive,
Sought help from friend and instructor
How to improve his drive,
Then qualified with a great round
Was razor sharp and keen,
And day and night was to be found
On driving range and green.

But when that ball was on the tee
He seemed to lose his grip,
And those around me did agree
The reason for the slip
Was when the Pro beside him came
He lost his nerve and pluck,
So lucky that I watched his aim
I had the time to duck!

FALLEN HERO

I knew a simple country boy
Who sang the cyclists' song of joy,
Each time they rode to victory
Upon a mountain top.

He told those who would lend an ear
Of brave men cycling without fear,
And they revelled in his story
As pure as a snow drop.

But the champ in yellow cheated
Soon his name would be deleted,
And he saw a fallen hero
He worshiped from the start.

Now he doesn't know who rides clean
Doubts men in yellow and in green,
And he cannot name a hero
With spirit in his heart.

Vote Michael Healy-Rae

(Election 2011)

It happened in the dead of night
When up a pole a young lad, bright
Removed a poster for the lark
And crossed the county bounds in dark.
From Kerry South to Cork North West
He brought the placard to suggest
To the electorate down his way
To vote for Michael Healy-Rae.

Next morning on his daily stroll
Tommy Joe saw up on a pole
A poster that looked out of place
But recognised the pleasant face.
There underneath the mug-shot fine
In writing bold, in grand design
Was a message for better pay,
Give number one to Healy-Rae.

Up on that pole with dapper cap
He looked a most studious chap
Who could stand up inside the Dail
And put it up to Fianna Fáil
Or any Taoiseach in debate
(Provided he got the mandate),
Yes anyone would earn their pay
To get the best of Healy-Rae.

The day of voting was at hand
And Tommy Joe was in demand,
He promised number one to all
Who canvassed him in pub and hall,
The ballot paper up and down
He scanned and flummoxed scratched his crown,
Saw none to please him on display
Wrote number one for Healy-Rae.

"Now the Captain's at the depot, lame but happy as a lark;
And in billets out in France men who knew him tell the story
Of 'the bloke that 'ad an accident when walking in the dark'-
While the captain teaches raw recruits the way to blood and glory."

From A Ballad by Siegfried Sassoon

The War Poems by Siegfried Sassoon is a revealing book of poems about the harrowing tales of World War 1. The above lines were penned on 25th October 1916. It tells a tale about a captain who shot himself in the foot in order to be sent home from the front line. Now he "teaches raw recruits the way to blood and glory."

Over the Top is inspired by Siegfried Sassoon's writing and tries to capture the love and devotion a young soldier has for his wife and young daughter. Writing to them what would be his final letter from the trenches on the night before he was killed in action during World War 1. Sadly this would have been just one of many letters sent home by young men before being killed in action.

OVER THE TOP

Letter from the Trenches.
(Somewhere in the Eastern front 1914)

This is the letter that he wrote
The night before he died,
They found it in his blood- soaked coat
With comrades there beside.

My Dear Roseanne, There is a pause
In fighting at the front,
I'm writing you this note because
Tomorrow we confront
The enemy with might and main
We're goin' over the top,
A thousand soldiers on the plain
With orders not to stop.

These past few weeks have been severe
On body, mind and soul,
The blizzards get you thinking queer
Down in this cubby-hole,
For five days now we are dug in
In bitter cold and snow,
It goes beyond a fellow's skin
At twenty plus below.

'Tis worst at night and to repose
My Dear I think of you,
In my mind's eye I see a rose
With perfume to imbue,
I see us walking hand in hand
Until up overhead,
The bombers come and on command
We shower them with lead.

What would I give to soak my skin
In water clean and warm?
The mud is really sticking in
Like pigs down on the farm.
My beard is rough, you wouldn't know
Me walking down the street,
But I'll scrub up as white as snow
My darling 'fore we meet.

How is lovely Donna Marie?
Does she remember Dad?
Why yesterday she was but three
In the trench I was sad,
But Bill the Gunner cheered me up
He poured a mug of rum,
And when we drank another cup
Old Bill began to hum.

At first 'twas like a lullaby
So soft was his refrain,

And then with a tear in his eye
He started up again,
His voice was deep and I could see
The Mississippi flow,
That Ol' Man River was to me
Worth more than gold you know.

We all joined in down in the trench
Sang Happy Birthday too,
And one boy sang his song in French
As sweet as honey dew,
Tell her that Dad did not forget
Her very special day,
For neither bomber nor bullet
Could stop us in our play.

Tis hard as hell to sleep at night
And dreams are all a daze,
I've seen brave men jump up with fright
Thinking they are ablaze,
The bangs, the blasts come thick and fast
And leave you all askew,
You never know which one is last
And that's the end of you.

Of course we pray and in the hole
We're all the same with God,
And every man here has a role
In boosting up the squad,

I've seen pictures of sweethearts pure
And men in warm embrace,
Praying that true love will endure
While tears roll down their face.

Of course we pray and in this hole
We're all the same with God.

And yet the day that we rolled up
In some forgotten town,
They cheered us like we won the cup
Having been two goals down,
And in the ruins and the smoke
They gathered round our tanks,
And with probity one man spoke
Said "Welcome" to the Yanks.

Like fireworks that light up the sky
Such joy can quickly pass,
I've seen brave comrades fight and die
Out in the field, alas,
And when you lose a treasured mate
You feel so lost inside,
You call on God to compensate
For part of you has died.

Sometimes at night it's good to cry
It drives the demons out,
For at the front to live or die
Can leave the best in doubt,
Here in the void men are devoid
Of love and tender care,
A mother's dish to be enjoyed
Would be beyond compare.

My darling, it is thoughts of you
That keeps the gloom away,
For I know when this war is through
We'll meet again some day,
By cotton fields once more we'll walk
In springtime and the fall,
At sunset we will sit and talk
With beauty to enthral.

I'm turning in, my dear, the pen
Is shaking in my hand,
Tomorrow with a thousand men
We're goin' to make a stand,
Over the top, we'll go, won't stop
Until this land is free,
Then come midnight with a teardrop
I'll write some more to thee.

GRANDAD'S COAT

Well Grandad gave that dog to me
When I was four and Jamie three,
That little pup with golden flecks
Was small and cute, we called him Rex,
He'd snuggle up beside the fire
When we were dressed in night attire,
Oh! how we got to love him so
And brought him with us to-and- fro.

Our Grandad loved that doggy too
Would throw a bone for him to chew,
Would sit for ages on a log
Talking kindly to our small dog,
Then Rex would sleep upon his lap
Or sometimes curl up in his cap,
And when he did go chase a fly
Grandad would laugh and wonder why.

Well we missed school that winter's day
When our Grandad just passed away,
Now I was nine and Jamie eight
We were both in a tearful state,
And Rex was clawing at the door
Looking for Grandad, Mama swore,
So we just took him on his lead
Though he was sad we both agreed.

But we bucked up as time went by
And on our doggy did rely
To fetch a ball or stick or rod
While on the neighbours' fields we trod,
Forever true, a faithful friend
Rex was a treasure till the end,
And for a whole week Jamie cried
When I told him that Rex had died.

Of course we were now in our teens
And growing up and wearing jeans,
We reminisced about the day
Grandad brought home that dog to stay,
And there was laughter through our tears
As we journeyed back through the years,
So we sat down and wrote a note
And buried Rex in Granddad's coat.

Happy Fellow

I knew a man back in my youth
Who whistled like a sparrow,
Oh he was good natured in truth
And daily pushed a barrow,
Around the yard with brush and spade
He made an honest living,
And though he was quite poorly paid
He made an art of smiling.

In that same yard in his posh car
The boss did drive with relish,
And he was wealthier by far
With houses two and snobbish,
He lived a life of luxury
Went to exotic places,
Ended up in the Treasury
Went weekly to the races.

I met them both in town last week
It startled me a little,
The boss was shuffling round and weak
It seems his bones are brittle,
My friend now draws the pension too
Still whistles like a sparrow,
And though his treasures they are few
He is a happy fellow.

I Never Thought I'd See The Day...

I never thought I'd see the day...
I used to hear the old folk say
      In meadows fair.
I never thought I'd see so soon
A man walking upon the moon
      Treading on air.

And when the television came
Their exclamations were the same
      All evening long.
I never thought I'd see Croke Park
From my kitchen or the skylark
      In fulsome song.

In youthful times I thought that this
Was babble that I should dismiss
      From aged men.
For everything was possible,
Every idea credible
      I figured then.

It's funny how the mindset stays
All too often set in its ways
      As life goes on.
And like those folk I used to know
My mind is now a trifle slow
When called upon.

Last week on an electric train
I found challenging to my brain
            To fathom out,
How up and down the track it went
Without a driver to prevent
            A crash or clout.

For where the driver should have sat
There were no gears for working at
            Or rod or stick.
I thought I'd never see the day
A train would move along this way,
            No Bob or Dick.

Unworthy Heir

Sometimes I think he's touched my soul,
Bob Service the great bard,
For like him I'm inclined to stroll
With a pen in the yard,
Scribbling on a postcard.

Why once or twice I've found a phrase
That suits my ditty fine,
But stopped from adding to my lays,
 Not sure if it were mine,
Had I stolen his line?

You see I read him all the time,
I know his verses well,
There is great beauty in his rhyme,
Oh how his stanzas jell,
They ring true like a bell.

I've read of 'Café de la Paix,'
And of 'The Black Fox Skin,'
Of 'Sam McGee' upon a sleigh,
'The Men That Don't Fit In,'
The sinner 'Hank the Finn.'

So when I read of "Dan McGrew"
Or howling wolf or bear,
Of lofty pine or caribou,
I feel his presence there,
Was I once to compare?

GOD'S GIFT

While sitting on a barber's chair
Trying to be polite,
I asked the girl cutting my hair
If her childhood was bright,
She looked at me with sparkling eyes
And said, "Oh it was fun,
Why I had lots of exercise
Out in the midday sun."

The pretty lass from way out east
Then put her scissors down,
"My youth," said she, "was quite a feast
Of laughter in our town,"
Her eyes lit up as she evoked
The nature of her play,
"'Twas like a carnival," she joked,
With new games every day."

Well I just sat there in my chair
And let the lass express,
Her musings on her Teddy Bear
Her dolly and her dress,
"Oh volley ball," said she, "was fun
And we had quite a team,
A tournament one year we won
When we did dare to dream."

Well by the time my hair was cut
The tears welled in my eyes,
I was brought back to tent and hut
And to mum's apple pies,
And yet that girl gave me a lift
For I thought in God's plan,
Childhood is such a special gift
Bestowed by him on man.

Old Stock

No queue stretching a half mile here
Just kindly neighbours calling by
With words of sympathy, sincere
A firm handshake, a hushed reply,
"She was a grand old age, thank God,
In good health till the very end,
I knew her when the road she trod
The long acre by Cary's bend."

No home for her away from home
Still the small house upon the hill,
Where she reluctant 'ere to roam
Baked apple tart each day to thrill,
In the small room now in repose
She slept for ninety years and four,
And smelt the fragrance of the rose
On summer mornings through the door.

"My Godmother," a woman prays
The tears still rolling down her face,
"How happy were my holidays
When you made me a shawl of lace,"
A sad farewell, a last goodbye
And then she steps out from the room,
The call to mourn, to unify
To see an old friend to the tomb.

"She was of old stock," said John Dee
The cortege shuffling down the street,
In satin now, her spirit free
To go where God and angels meet,
"She was of old stock," said John Browne
Taking his turn beneath the oak,
And as they laid her coffin down
"It was fitting,"the village spoke.

CHRISTMAS IN JULY

The room was desolate and bare
A bed, a press, a sink, a chair
And I a visitor sat there
In silence.

My eyes wandered around the room
I spoke in jest to lift the gloom
'Twas July with flowers in bloom
Resplendent.

Oh he was lucid now and then
But most things he had forgotten
I recalled names which did gladden
Him greatly.

I saw a tear come to his eye
It was two years since I'd stopped by
I did my best to bring him joy
And laughter.

We didn't speak about the crash
A vibrant life changed in a flash
Back in our youth we wielded ash
Together.

My eyes fixed on the window sill
A Christmas card on display still
I looked at it, his eyes did fill
With wonder.

A Christmas card in mid-July
"He just got one," the nurse stopped by
"So many friends he had," said I
In sorrow.

RECALLING BESS

Strange how some things don't change at all
Was taken back today,
To my dear father's milking stall
One wet and windy May,
It must be fifty years I guess
Before I went to school,
I had to milk the white cow Bess
On a three-legged stool.

Well I was slow and Mam was quick
And Dad was in between,
Old Bess was calm would never kick
That was left to Róisín,
But sometimes Bess would swish her tail
And hit me on the mug,
While looking back from in the bale
And killing some poor bug.

Then up at school a friend would say
"Forgot to wash your face?"
Then right across to my dismay
A streak of green I'd trace,
And as I'd rub my sleeve over
I'd just transfer the streak,
Put cow dung on my pullover
For the rest of the week.

This morning it wasn't old Bess
Perhaps her progeny,
Across my face with great success
Her tail swished into me,
And as I sat down for breakfast
With everything in place,
My daughter looked at me aghast
Said "Go and wash your face!"

NEW FACE AT THE A.A

Well I was in the room that night a broken man and
beat,
And nothing in the world it seemed could save me
from defeat,
Though I had fallen many times I felt this time was
last,
For like the dreary winter days the light was fading
fast.
I'd emptied out my pockets and I'd emptied out my
soul,
And nothing seemed to matter now, life was beyond
control,
The courage I had mustered up like the last train was
gone,
And all because of the damn booze the sunshine never
shone.

There we all sat around the room my broken friends
and me
While listening to each other's tales of want and
misery,
And though each man a shadow was of what he might
have been,
We did our best to figure out why life became ob-
scene.
Then while we talked a man slipped in and posed
upon the floor,

With mask and gown, a fearful frown, he gently
closed the door,
We were aghast to see him there a surgeon of renown,
All we could do was nod our heads and bid him to sit
down.

Well his hands shook and as he took the mask down
from his face,
The tears rolled down his working gown and we felt
out of place,
"I'm here," said he, "so you can see that I have lived a
lie,
I'm not the man you thought I was," and we did not
reply,
"I'm just a fraud so don't applaud the work I've done,"
said he,
"I'm tired and weak, the future's bleak," he told us tearfully.
As he sat down upon the chair each one of us in turn
Went up to him and shook his hand to show him our
concern.

Of course I knew the way he felt, I was that soldier
too,
The entire world just tumbles down and comrades
they are few,
When deep inside the emptiness turns into deep
despair,
Your nerves are raw and you can't draw on strength
that isn't there,

And that one drink when on the brink will leave you like a thief,
For comforts sought will bring you nought except heartache and grief,
We've all been there and friend I swear there's nothing but a mess
When the crowd leave you sit and grieve, don't know your own address.

A block layer of sorts that's me, at school I wasn't bright,
The surgeon with the med' degree came to my room that night,
We sat and talked and then we walked along the avenue,
We found a seat where he did treat me to a tale or two.
I guess the booze is just the same for every Joe and Bob,
The surgeon that sat beside me was renowned at his job,
A year before when at death's door, he fixed up Tom my friend,
When everyone around the town said he would never mend.

It's funny how you can buck up when thinking of another,
I stopped thinking about myself, instead thought of my brother,

And bit by bit his head was cleared of work and stress and drink,
And maybe I played a small part dragging him from the brink.
I guess that I am kind of chuffed I was the friend he chose,
He draws from me and me from him and that's the way it goes,
We both stay clear of wine and beer just one day at a time,
And though we know progress is slow, we say faith is no crime.

It is a dream the little stream where we both like to fish,
And now and then upon the bank we cook a tasty dish,
We don't talk shop instead we swap rich tales from long ago,
In the same league as my colleague? Gosh no, I'm way below,
But my reward is on the ward where he works late at night,
With expertise to cure disease and make a future bright,
The hands that shook the night he came are now nimble and free,
That he can cure folk of their pain is good enough for me.

Prayer At Milking Time

Dear Lord, help me to remain true
To my calling to the land,
So that in everything I do
I can see your guiding hand,
Help me to reap that which I sow
Be content with my return,
That I might plough a straight furrow
'Neath a hill of golden fern.

Make me aware of the beauty
Of the pasture rich and fair,
To be mindful of my duty
To animals in my care,
Let there be a safe passage through
For all creatures great and small,
And grant me, Lord, a bird's-eye view
Of the wonder of them all.

When I am tired in need of rest
Let forbearance keep me strong,
At evening time let me be blessed
To the land may I belong,
In fields of daisies let me sit
With restful cows providing
Solace for my benefit
Pure stillness there residing.

Make me aware of the beauty
Of the pasture rich and fair

When my time comes to pension off
Grant that my son will follow,
And happily rest on a trough
Admiring hill and hollow,
My father's father owned the land
Turned it into fertile soil,
Lord grant that those with pen in hand
Our livelihood will not spoil.

THE BUTTERFLY

Oh I have seen the butterfly
And I have seen the mountain high
And I have seen the summer sky
So blue.
And I have seen the lordly pine
And grappled with a fishing line
Beside a small stream so divine
And true.

And I have seen the leaping trout
And water trickling from a spout
And small waves rushing in and out
At shore.
And I have heard the cuckoos call
And sat beside a waterfall
Have been enchanted by it all
And more.

And I have seen the sunset red
And swallows flying overhead
And little calves so spirited
In flight.
And I have seen the rainbows glow
And donkeys laze in the meadow
The moon shining down on the snow
At night.

And I have seen a hundred ways
The Good Lord brightens up my days
So on my knees I give him praise
That's due.
But most of all when floating by
I've seen the one who is so shy
The stately looking butterfly
Yes I have seen the butterfly
Have you?

YEARNINGS

Such beauty as the autumn trees
In memory's enshrined,
At leisure picking blackberries
Comes rushing to my mind,
When autumn winds blow in my face
And birds pitch high and low,
I love old footsteps to retrace
With nostalgia and slow.

And then from bushes wild and free
I fill up to the top,
A jar like my Mam gave to me
With two pence for the shop,
How sweet the berries taste there still
Like when I was a boy,
They bring back memories to thrill
My ageing heart with joy.

'Twas fast I picked the berries then
And rushed back home to Mam,
Who used gifts sent down from heaven
To turn the fruit to jam,
And on white cake at supper time
I spread it thick and wide,
Like Snow White in the pantomime
My heart was filled with pride.

JUPITER

While driving home one winter's night
Said my small girl to me,
"See dad the stars are shining bright
As bright as bright can be,"
And I looked up and saw the stars
A million of them shine,
Like butterflies, caterpillars
They were hers, they were mine.

"And do you know the brightest star
Is Jupiter," said she,
"It shines down on us from afar
On mountain, vale and sea,"
She pointed to it in the sky
Was enthralled by its glow,
And I could see her eager eye
Gaze out through the window.

We journeyed on at modest speed
Chatted with gay accord,
And to her musings I paid heed
Her spirit I adored,
And when the star faded from view
Behind a tree or hill,
She waited for it to shine through
Bright as a daffodil.

And all along the country road
She said 'twas getting near,
I had my doubts the way it glowed
That Jupiter was here,
My mind was filled with joy and praise
For her engaging mind,
And I thanked God she filled my days
With blessings of this kind.

When nearing home we found it was
A light above the wood,
But I encouraged her because
Her interest was good,
We went down to the village green
Gazed at the Milky Way,
Yes Jupiter alright was queen
My small girl had her say.

CROWING

Upon the Empire State Building
I was resting one day,
Oh it was exhilarating
Just like a matinee,
The New York skyline was a treat
Majestic to the view,
And I could see down to Wall Street
And up Fifth Avenue.

We had queued for an hour or more
To get on to the lift
That took us to the viewing floor
Oh it was very swift,
Well down below each motor car
Was minute to the eye,
The Hudson was sweetest by far
As it went rolling by.

Tourists were there from everywhere
From China to Japan,
Some looked to be walking on air
Like the cameraman,
"It is a wonder of the world,"
A stranger said to me,
"A work of genius unfurled"
And I had to agree.

Just then I fixed upon a crow
Quite placid and sedate,
The bird seemed to be in the know
About the Empire State,
He wasn't in the least put out
By the sight-seeing crowd,
But sat there looking all about
Conceited like and proud.

He seemed to say, "Why all the fuss?
I come here every day,
See I can fly to any truss
And come back here to play,
There is no building in this state
That I can't scale at ease,
See watch me and I'll demonstrate,"
He flew off in the breeze.

Towards Ellis Island he did fly
And it occurred to me,
The skyscraper quarter mile high
Was to him like a tree,
The feast of engineering skill
We had just come to know,
Was just another routine drill
For the conceited crow.

THE BY-ELECTION

Good men and true of every hue
Come listen to my tale
Concerning Dan a gentleman
Who liked to sup his ale,
Around these parts were broken hearts
When a T.D. passed on,
Though hardly cold when folk were told
Of a by-election.

The campaigning was absorbing
In village street and hall,
And those who wrote said that the vote
Was far too close to call,
In every bar familiar
The party line was spun,
And drink was bought by those who sought
The precious number one.

In our saloon one afternoon
A candidate stopped by,
Oh she was fair with golden hair
The type to catch your eye,
She cut a dash with plenty cash
To garner every vote,
And Dan felt good and so he should
With the cure for his throat.

All of that week with tongue in cheek
Dan lots of blarney spun,
Upon his coat it said to vote
For Myra number one,
With pint in hand he took a stand
And called for change all round,
The blonde bombshell had cast her spell
And soon she would be crowned.

When pubs change hands if it demands
There is a hooley held,
And at our inn which was changing
Good drinkers they were felled,
Before midnight it was a sight
The changing of the guard,
And Dan was there 'sleep on a chair
And with his voting card.

Next day arrived he was revived
'Twas the day of the vote,
At half past nine and feeling fine
He went to get his coat,
The new barman said "Come here, Dan
And have a pint on me,"
With drinks galore and an encore
Dan stayed till half past three.

He staggered out and with a shout
Said "Give her number one,
The lovely lass who has got class
She will not be undone,"
Then into bed to clear his head
He went before the vote,
Fell fast asleep all in a heap
While still wearing his coat.

When he awoke and had a soak
He headed for the school
His vote to cast, he was aghast,
Left looking quite a fool,
He'd slept all night it was a fright
He'd missed out by a day,
The tally men with pad and pen
Had Myra on her way.

CHAINED

It's no big deal for me and Jane
To go into a bar,
And sit and talk on things mundane
For that's the way things are.
A father and his daughter just
In regular discourse,
Where love is shared and joy and trust
And fun are uppermost.

She sat beside us that fine day
Looked tired and weak and wan,
While both of us were talking gay
Her joy in life was gone,
"We don't agree, you know," said she
And shed a lonely tear,
"My father lost respect for me-
I frequented the pier."

The contrast between her and Jane
Was same as black and white,
Scars on her hands revealed the pain
She lacked the will to fight,
It's no big deal for me and Jane
To go into a bar,
But when you see such hurt and pain,
A lass tied to an endless chain,
Your thoughts are lost afar.

SACKED

Lo Mary Kate is talking to
Her hubby on the ladder,
She tells him curtly what to do
And she is getting madder,
The paint he's spattered on the wall
He has got quite an earful,
He's nervous in case he will fall
So he is extra careful.

The paint is on the window sill
He dips into the gallon,
He paints the wall with little skill
He will get no blue-ribbon,
"Hold on to the ladder," he calls,
"For it is feeling shaky,"
"You're streaking it," to him she bawls,
"Already it is flaky."

The corner boys are whistling now
They know there is commotion,
They love it when there is a row
It adds to the emotion,
Pale Primrose is the latest hue
To decorate her dwelling,
And when the painting's at issue
The outcome is compelling.

The house is turning out all right
But Mary Kate's not happy,
And while her husband is polite
She is peevish and snappy,
In an instant he's coming down
She has sacked him, her painter,
And while she paints the windows brown
He holds on to the ladder.

The Man Behind the Shades

He never saw the flowers grow in spring
Or in wintertime the snowfall dazzling,
And when he was a child he didn't know
The difference between flowers and snow.

Until his father took him to a field
Where the fragrance of flowers was revealed,
Then by a rippling stream they did repose
Where he felt the cool water on his toes.

He knew that birds sang out each day with glee
Since first he heard them on his granddad's knee,
But never did he see the lark or thrush
The robin or the swallow on a bush.

Though he was blessed when he did learn to play
Music which was a gift to him each day,
Through his music the darkness turned to light
Helped to compensate for the gift of sight.

For he found when his fingers brushed the keys
It was like being in amongst the trees,
And in a while there flowed to him the words
Of songs that spoke of love and peace and birds.

His voice was like the crispness of the morn'
Refreshing and as golden as the corn,
And though his skin was dark just like the shades
That covered up his eyes the accolades

Greeted him each time he performed on stage
And he became an icon of an age,
He sang songs that extolled the fatherland
And young folk joined in with him hand in hand.

And older folk were sometimes moved to tears
When the music and words rolled back the years,
He carried an expression on his face
That those people who loved him did embrace.

He went to places none of them had been
And sang of places none of them had seen,
And though his eyes were hidden from the glare
His face lit up with warmth beyond compare.

Though he was blind the people recognised
The sense beyond the norm he vocalized,
It seemed to them he saw much more than they
When he took up the stool, began to play.

Thus was the gift of music to him given
Just as the gift of sight from him was taken,
The poor black boy who never saw the birds
Grew up to be a man of special words.

The poor black boy who never saw a rose
Had his name in bright lights at city shows,
Behind the shades he hit the notes each night
With eyes that could not see but still were bright.

THE TENOR IN THE CHURCH

They found him on a park side bench one cold
December morn',
'Twas sixty years that very day since my friend Rob
was born,
They found him with his rosary, a bottle there beside,
And no one saw the falling star the moment that he
died.
And no one mourned his passing for he was a down
and out,
Whose mind was torn between extremes of self-
reproach and doubt,
They brought him to Saint Mary's and I went along
that day,
You see back home in our small town the two of us
used play.

But that was fifty years ago when we played at
football,
And kicked the leather to and fro and over Reilly's wall,
Up on his back I'd stand and jump a half dozen times
over,
Retrieve the ball with a great thump from that fine
field of clover.
Rob grew to be a strapping lad, who could reach to
the sky,
And pluck a ball from the kick out and then electrify
With passes to the left and right as down the wing he stole,

"Johnsie,"he'd call me, "show out right, you'll get the winning goal."

That winning team was not the same when Rob left
over night,
You see we missed his mighty frame, his talent to
excite,
Some said that he was due a rise down on Bob
Connor's farm
Where he worked since he was a boy with strong and
steady arm.
But others said that he knew well that it could never be,
That he and Kate, Bob Connor's girl could wed and
live carefree,
So at the AGM that year there was sadness all round,
When to us all it became clear Rob was not
homeward bound.

Christmases came and summers too but Rob did not
return,
We missed him on the football field, with horse and
cart and churn,
Some rumours spread around the town about his state
in life,
And talk about him wandering near Shepherds Bush
was rife.
After my playing days were o'er I joined the exiles
boat,
And bid farewell to my home place with a lump in

my throat,
But on my way to London town I vowed that I would find
The long lost pal that I had known to be faithful and kind.

One Christmas Eve while my kids played I packed into a box
Some bread and cake that my wife made, a woolly vest and socks,
A jumper that I bought for him, a bottle of fine rum,
And made my way to Shepherds Bush where I found my old chum.
It broke my heart to see him there upon the park side bench,
With three or four of his new mates and a great thirst to quench,
Said he, "we haven't met before" when I called out his name,
I left the box - it shocked me so to see his drooping frame.

Sometimes I saw him round the Bush or subway late at night,
I never looked him in the eye, which would not be polite,
I'd leave a burger on the bench, a bottle on the ground,
I didn't need no evidence; I knew they would be found.

How strange it was a sergeant rang from cross the
Irish Sea,
Telling me that my friend had died and he dressed
scantily,
They traced him with a medal that he won in sixty
four,
He took it from around his neck and he at heaven's
door.

Well there inside Saint Mary's church the tears rolled
down my face,
There was but ten penniless souls in God's own
dwelling place,
Where was the choir that I'd heard sing with harmony
before?
Where were the pall bearers to bring my old pal
through the door?
I made my way to the top pew and nodded to the
priest,
I whispered that with his consent I'd talk for the
deceased,
Well friend, I am no orator, but I spoke from the
heart,
About the boy who loved football - who drove the
horse and cart.

Who ploughed the land with spirit grand, who sat
upon a stool
And milked ten shorthorn cows by hand on summer

For blessed are the poor of heart.

mornings cool,

Who had a dream that turned to nought, his spirit broke in two,

And in the comfort that he sought he lost the life he knew.

Like disciples they looked at me those ten scarecrows of men,

And in their eyes 'twas plain to see that they were all done in,

I told them that they would meet Rob one day at heaven's door,

For blessed are the poor of heart - I felt their spirits soar.

Then as we raised his coffin high, those down and outs and me,

A voice sang out from down the church with grace and sanctity,

A tenor voice that had us all stand transfixed on the aisle,

And when I looked him in the eye I saw my old friend's smile.

The snowflakes fell upon the pine; we lowered him to the clay,

I enquired of the tenor man if he were here to stay,

"I'm flying home tonight," said he with dignity and charm,

"You see he was my father who worked on my granddad's farm."

LETTER FROM MIA

Well Mia wrote a letter to Grandad in Dublin town,
Said, "Grandad it is about time that you were coming down,
We haven't seen you for a while and guess you'd never know
How I am wishing I could move out from big sister Jo,
She's always teasing me in bed and pulling at the clothes,
And Grandad bet you won't believe she even picks her nose,
And when I told mum all of this Jo said it was just lies,
I promise if you do come down I'll bake you apple pies."

Well Grandad got his tool box out and boarded the first train,
And down to Cork he went next day in all the wind and rain,
And at the station he was met by Mia and her mum,
He said that he could not believe how big she had become,
Before Mia was out of bed and up at play next morn,
She heard hammering overhead where the roof had been worn,
There Grandad was making a room up in the attic space,
He whispered to her at lunchtime "soon you'll have your own
place."

There wasn't such excitement since she started at play school,
And one by one she asked Grandad to name her every tool,
She only saw him at mealtime for he was up above,
She made a card and sent it up, "To Grandad with my love,"
The timber came in a big truck, the attic window too,
And Grandad said it was her luck that she'd have such a view,
She said she'd want at least one shelf to carry her new books,
Grandad she said, "Now don't forget at least two or three hooks."

Each night Grandad met with his friends to drink a pint of beer,
And told of Mia's attic room with good humour and cheer,
The more they asked the more it seemed to light that Grandad's eyes,
He loved to tell the barman about Mia's apple pies,
The stairs then came and was put in and up went a new bed,
And Grandad painted the new room with pale primrose and red,
And Mum bought her a brand new quilt and Dad gave her a hug
The first night that she climbed the stairs to see her bright new rug.

At last she was in her new room and Jo shared her delight,
For she knew she could make her plans for her room the next night,
Grandad was there to tuck her in and Mum and Dad as well,
And Mia said her new room was better than a hotel,
"But Grandad," she said, "Over here I cannot see the moon,"
He changed her bed and overhead 'twas like a great balloon,
And as she looked up at the sky the small girl fell asleep,
And to the window Grandad went just for a little peep.

Next evening he was on the train at ease and with much pride,
While Mia looked up at the stars from her new room inside,
And in the post a letter came, said "Grandad you are best
For making a new room for me that's cosy as a nest,
For the new shelf and the new desk, the picture on the wall,
Why Mum said she had one the same way back when she was small,
I'll never know how you could think of such a great idea,
Mum's getting a new border, pink, With Love to You, From Mia."

THE DAY GOD CRIED IN HEAVEN
For my brothers and sisters who died on 9/11

The Lord was resting up that day
In his garden retreat,
He heard a report far away
That brought him to his feet,
His angels gathered round his side
Consoled him everyone,
They told him many souls had died
Great carnage had been done.

The Lord relived his Calvary
And looked down from above,
He thought of how in Galilee
He preached of peace and love,
He wondered about the free will
Bestowed on human kind
His father's duty to fulfil
The ways of God to bind.

As the Towers did tumble down
The Lord knelt down to pray,
And tears fell on his dressing gown
In heaven on that day,
"Oh how I tire of evil ways,"
Thought he in great distress,
"Why must there be discord always
Not peace and forgiveness?"

A fireman slowly came to view
With numbness and despair,
And as he saw him Jesus knew
 He had a hero there,
"Forgive me, Lord," the fireman said,
"For wrongs that I have done,"
The Master's arms around him spread
His healing had begun.

Each victim there the Lord embraced
And gave them angels wings,
And every hero was showcased
And showered with blessings,
And as their spirits floated round
With energy and grace,
The joy they now felt was profound
In God's own dwelling place.

As God looked down on Ground Zero
He felt the world stand still,
There everyone was a hero
In the rubble and chill,
And as he watched a city mourn
He was renewed with pride,
Though battered, weary and forlorn
Its spirit had not died.

A HUNDRED YEARS FROM NOW

When I was young and troubled by
My lessons up at school,
And something hard would make me cry
I'd sit there on the stool,
My Dad would say "sure life's a game
Son don't you worry now,
Remember 'twill be all the same
A hundred years from now."

When I left home for the first time
I was homesick and sad,
Each night I'd take out at bedtime
A letter from my Dad,
It cheered me up to see his name
When the lights did allow,
He'd write "it will be all the same
A hundred years from now."

I didn't heed his sound advice
Till I got on in years,
Now I use it as a device
To save heartbreak and tears,
To be temperate is my aim
To keep sweat off my brow,
Remembering 'twill be the same
A hundred years from now.

So any time that my young boys
Find they are in a stew,
And life is not full of the joys
I go and make a brew,
I tell them life is just a game
It cheers them up somehow,
To know it will be all the same
A hundred years from now.

THE CELTIC TIGER

I noticed them around the street
On their way to the bank,
Entrepreneurs who looked complete
So polished like and swank,
With brief cases they swaggered past
Carried plans to excite,
Just after a business breakfast
Or coming from a site.

Well my deposit was modest
The Tiger passed my gate,
But seeing I made it honest
I still laughed with my mate,
For folk like me just plod along
Not yearning to excite,
You'll hear us sing the same old song
Each morning, noon and night.

But I was downcast one fine day
When there inside the bank,
The manager hailed straightaway
An entrepreneur swank,
Thought I the bus has taken off
And I am left behind,
By every zealous man and toff
And tycoon of that kind.

They built houses in every town
Apartments on each hill,
And office blocks of red and brown
(Why most are empty still),
A millionaire could well be found
Inside the village store,
Fellows who never had a pound
Were made for evermore.

The Celtic Tiger came and went
What is the state of play?
I have enough to pay the rent
And for a drink today,
The managers gave out too much
It all ended in tears,
Entrepreneurs were out of touch
We'll foot the bill for years!

The Last Days of the Boom

From the East they came like The Three Wise Men,
Not bearing gifts or following a star,
But following the boom they heard of when
Villagers sang of gold in fields afar.
Nor were they wise or versed in worldly ways,
A youth of labour spent without reward,
The same old landmarks, the same weary days,
The same grubby hands in the dank steelyard.

And when they came they settled in our town,
We were glad to get our share of the boom,
They kept the house they stayed in upside-down,
'Twas said they shared half dozen to a room.
They revelled in the money that they made,
Drank pure vodka like water from a spout,
It was like they were on a last crusade
With nothing in the world to care about.

And side by side we worked with them on site,
Building houses where farmers used to plough,
We believed that the boom was watertight,
We thought of nothing but the here and now.
Our new buddies were eager volunteers,
Taking orders they didn't understand,
Nor did they know who were the profiteers
Or the value of the notes in their hand.

We did our best to help them on the way,
Gave them apple tart and scones for a treat,
But they drank like they were on holiday,
Perhaps it was a symptom of defeat.
We were told that thousands more would arrive,
The future would be brighter than the past,
And in our town 'twas good to be alive,
For every day was better than the last.

By the estate there's a wall built with stone,
Testimony of skill and expertise,
I t was built with great resolve and backbone,
By those workers with a yearning to please.
But work dried up around the building sites,
And one by one the comrades slipped away,
No more would we watch them on summer nights
Go up and down like shoppers on their way.

They left it late to make their pot of gold,
The boom was all but over when they came,
They are owed lots in wages we are told,
Sadly avarice extinguished the flame.
And now when they return to the steel yard
They talk about their time spent far away,
Of how they worked for weeks without reward
And apple tart was sweeter than the pay.

DON'T LET THE FIRE GO OUT

Take off that frown you are in charge
Your wife is out today,
Her batteries she will recharge,
You'll chop the wood you say,
Now don't forget to feed the dog
He's scampering about,
Put on the grate a cheery log
Don't let the fire go out.

Get off your butt it's getting late
Collect the kids from school,
They're waiting for you at the gate
One's at the swimming pool,
Heat up their mash and cut a dash
There is no need to shout,
And when you're done put out the trash
Don't let the fire go out.

You've watched the game a dozen times
Why press replay once more?
Now you are paying for your crimes
Get up and brush the floor,
Then see that homework is well done
And if you are in doubt,
Go right back to where you've begun
Don't let the fire go out.

You have messed up, that's nothing new
Your wife will soon be home,
Then there will be hullabaloo
Best pray to Saint Jerome,
Put a nice log down on the fire
She cannot do without,
It is the seat of her desire,
Beside it she loves to retire,
Don't let the fire go out!

CROCODILE TEARS

Her spouse had died, she cried and cried
For hours on end that day,
No priest or friend her heart could mend
Her grief was there to stay,
Her Jack was gone, the one who shone
In good times and in bad,
She'd surely miss his hug, his kiss
She was forlorn and sad.

Well hundreds came to praise his name
Pay respects that were due,
Through woeful tears she recalled years
When life had true value,
All dressed in black she did not lack
Decorum up at mass,
For down the aisle she cried all while
Jack's coffin there did pass.

In the graveyard oh it was hard
For the young widow there,
When Jack went down in the clay brown
She found it hard to bear,
In dizzy pose she threw a rose
Down after the deceased,
She almost went where Jack was sent
Her wailing never ceased.

Now bleary-eyed from the graveside
She was led by the hand,
Words in her ear helped her eyes clear
When the crowd did disband,
The undertaker, cabinetmaker
Had his sight set on Jill,
He called her honey, gave back some money
The night she paid the bill.

After six weeks, blusher on cheeks
She was in church once more,
Now up the aisle in lovely style
Walked Jill to smiles galore,
Then on her hand a wedding band
The new widow was wed,
But down her way wise folk will say
Her Jack would have seen red!

Preview to next 2 Poems

The following two poems were inspired by two very different set of circumstances. Bill McLaren was born in Hawick in Scotland in 1923 and in 1953 made his national debut as a commentator for BBC Radio. Until his retirement in 2002 he was known as "the voice of rugby". The great Welsh player Gareth Edwards said of him "That lovely border dialect of Bill's has transcended the game for thirty or forty years".

In this tribute to Bill I have tried to capture the effect that distinctive border dialect had on me as a young boy after listening to him commentate on radio or on black and white television. Just like Micheal O'Hehir in Gaelic Games and Peter O'Sullivan in Horse Racing, Bill was a legend in his time.

The second poem After All-Ireland Glory was written after I came across a photograph of Michaela Harte just about to embrace her father Tyrone Gaelic Football manager Mickey Harte following the team's success in the 2005 All Ireland football final. It struck a chord because just like Michaela who travelled with her dad to many games and training sessions my youngest son Philip has been a constant companion with me while coaching football teams. There is no sweeter moment than the moment the final whistle is blown and the team has been successful. For dad and daughter it must surely have been a blissful moment.

THE VOICE OF RUGBY
Bill McLaren 1923-2010

Before I knew the meaning of passion
His voice had already embraced my soul,
For it was filled with warmth and emotion
When a thistle wearing Scot dropped a goal,
Before I heard of Rangers or Celtic,
I had heard of Bill McLaren the Scot
Whose phrases filled the airways like magic
In commentaries clear as a snap shot.

Before I saved up for a rugby ball
I used the bottle mother had for quix,
And I would kick conversions o'er the stall
The same way Tommy Kiernan took his kicks,
I would be Bill McLaren I recall
And Mike Gibson and Willie John McBride,
I'd commentate while running with the ball
And get the winning score away out wide.

His genius was a pleasure to behold,
It mesmerized me when I was a boy,
That dialect was as precious as gold
And to this day it fills my heart with joy,
If I were Gavin Hastings, Barry John,
Bill Beaumont, J.P.R., or Jackie Kyle,
I'd go and put some old recordings on
And listen to Bill call my name with style.

Impartial, yes and friend and foe alike
Were seduced by his melodious tones,
For when he took his seat behind the mike
You got a pleasant feeling in your bones,
You knew the son of Hawick would rouse up
The passion in your heart like dynamite,
With sayings as pure as a buttercup,
He made the ball spin faster when in flight.

In days when boys were men before their time,
And players kicked and scrummaged in the mud,
Bill invented commentary in rhyme,
That swept through rugby fields just like a flood,
And me well when I played out in the yard
I'd imitate his brogue with great delight,
"Yes Willie John has got his just reward
They'll be singing in the valleys tonight."

AFTER ALL-IRELAND GLORY
25 September2005
Remembering Michaela

'Twas the moment when two hearts met
In victory with pride,
The summit of their feelings yet
The triumph of a side
That he had moulded into one
With mastery and class,
And she had seen how it was done
Could recall every pass.

'Twas the moment he saw her smile
With love and admiration,
In the glow she embraced him while
He roused up half the nation,
And in the din he heard her say
"I'm so proud of you Dad,
All-Ireland champions today
Oh what a time we've had."

'Twas the moment when he recalled
The journeys into night
With his wee girl who was enthralled
By a football in flight,
And she who blossomed like a rose
Helped him to lead the way,
She was his rock, the one he chose
To teach him how to pray.

'Twas the moment when love flowed through
Them pure as sparkling water,
And in his wisdom there he knew
He had a special daughter,
For in the moment that they shared
After All-Ireland glory,
He knew she loved him, knew she cared
Was central to his story.

WHEN ONLY ONE CAME BACK

For Pods'

He gave his all and maybe more
Than they did understand,
For he had been this way before
Had made the Promised Land
With teams he moulded well into
A fashion of his own,
Who from him inspiration drew
He was their corner stone.

They'd have to go the extra mile
He knew what that entailed,
He promised it would be worthwhile
Teams with big heart prevailed,
He led them to the mountain top
On one fine summer's night,
The feeling there they would not swap
They said he did unite.

But he was getting on in age
New ideas were heard,
Not lacking honour or courage
He left without a word,
And of the thirty that he drilled
Only one boy came back,
To thank him for the way he thrilled,
For keeping him on track.

And it reminded him of God
Who ten lepers did heal,
When on the path of life he trod
But only one did feel
True gratitude and thoughtfulness
To come and bow his head,
And in his heart he too did bless
The one who scripture read.

THE BLACK DOG

He wakes to find the emptiness inside
The thoughts of gloominess intensified,
He lies in bed and stares around the room
Dejected by the weariness and gloom,
He must get up for work and face the day
Already happy folk are on their way,
He falls asleep still struggling for control
The Black Dog has returned to stalk his soul.

It's half past nine when he wakes up once more
Feels worthless as he steps out on the floor,
He wonders what beset him in the night
That robbed him of the feelings of delight,
What rekindled the ashes of despair
Asking questions when answers aren't there,
He cuts the sticks half sleepy in the shed
Then wearily he goes back to his bed.

He sleeps once more his mind is numb and
scarred
Like a drifter at night in a blizzard,
He yearns for the desire to work and play
But lacks the will that's necessary today,
He feels like he's a zombie in the bed
For his brain is so weary and knotted,
While he's asleep he is released from pain
Unaware of the turmoil in his brain.

The phone rings by his bed at two or three
A phone call from one of the family,
He speaks with steady voice into the phone
He has calmed down the Black Dog with a bone,
This is his secret and he will not tell
Even his closest friend that he's in hell,
He pours a cup of tea to clear the fog
Everything helps when fighting the Black Dog.

It's evening time the guilt within him grows
For wasting a good day beneath the clothes,
He casts a glance up at the elder tree
But knows that for the moment he's not free,
There is a barricade he must remove
Before the spirit in him can improve,
He rests awhile upon the garden gate
Pities himself for being in this state.

The curtain's up inside the village hall
A patriot he is and does enthral,
It's like another man is in his place
With confidence written across his face,
A contradiction surely it must be
To camouflage the Black Dog totally,
On his way home he's feeling not so bad
And ponders on the sense of feeling sad.

Once more the veil comes down while he's asleep
Leaves him with mood black as a chimney sweep,
He lies in bed observing it awhile
And prays to God to help bring him a smile,
The sun shines brightly but he doesn't care
Just looking to find comfort from somewhere,
He does his jobs more sprightly in the yard
A glint of radiance is his reward.

But still he finds it hard to concentrate
Wishes with all his heart to extirpate
The blackness and the darkness and the gloom
The melancholy flowing through the room,
The lack of energy and drive and zest
The feeling of lethargy after rest,
The feeling of despair misunderstood
The constant analysing of childhood.

Once more he sleeps and wakes to greet the day
In somewhat better mood for work and play,
The Black Dog no longer snarls at his heels
And in the morning sun a smile he steals,
He knows the worst is over, is relieved
To find the joy of living is retrieved,
For bit by bit the sadness ebbs away
Although he knows it will return some day.

The Black Dog comes and goes and all awhile
He's learned to come back fighting with a smile,
He doesn't fight or strike out with a blow
Instead he's learned to drift on with the flow,
When days are good with a smile on his face
He works with joy but cuts down on the chase,
On other days while struggling through the fog
He lives in the shadow of the Black Dog.

GET UP AND GO

In days when you have nought to do
You've lost your job and pride,
You sit and stare, don't even care
Your self esteem has died,
Get up and go where small streams flow
Into a course or swell,
You've read from books, you have good looks
Young man you have done well.

The hilltops green, the vales between
Are waiting for your call,
The lark and thrush are on the bush,
The stunning waterfall,
The lordly pine is yours and mine,
The sunset ever red,
The winter snow and the rainbow
Will raise your drooping head.

Find a small church where you can search
For peace and calm and more,
In this retreat you will defeat
Your demons and restore
Your faith and pride for deep inside
Are values you hold high,
Go talk the talk and walk the walk
And carry on with joy.

You've lost your job, you're short a bob
See still the pine trees grow,
You're a good man, part of God's plan
Don't plough a lone furrow,
Be brave and leave the things that peeve
Go search for greater thrills,
The sun will rise to your surprise
Beyond the distant hills.

Puppy Love

My little pup you are so gay
This lovely summer's night,
I'm watching you at fun and play
You fill me with delight,
What joy you bring to me at ease
Watching the sunset glow,
You do not know how to displease
Out here in the meadow.

You look to me for stimulus
And then you scamper round,
Your escapades are mischievous
On hilltop green and mound,
And now I see you jump with verve
Over the tufts of grass,
And round about you twist and swerve
Until my seat you pass.

Then with a bounce you're in my lap
And snuggling up to me,
But in a jiff you're out the gap
And running wild and free,
Come back to me you speedy pup
Or you'll get lost you know,
Take time to see the buttercup
And watch the sunset glow.

Ah now you hear me calling out
With ears pricked in the air
You hurry back steadfast and stout
Almost fast as a hare,
Your escapades are a handful
For an old chap like me,
Although my life would be quite dull
Without our repartee.

Ho Ho I'm lying on my back
And looking into space,
Hey puppy good manners you lack
Please stop licking my face,
Alright it is a sign of love
That I should be so blessed,
To have birds singing up above
And you at my behest.

That's good my pup you're on a lead
We're at a sober pace,
Now don't you pull at me I plead
For this is not a race,
You're panting and it's no surprise
You haven't stopped all day,
We've both had lots of exercise
We've both had lots of play.

CHEAT

Have you heard about the athlete
Who won gold on the track?
To better his time and compete
Kept a syringe and pack.

He shed a tear for righteousness
As the flag was raised high,
And took the gold with graciousness
As music filled the sky.

The medal now is in a vault
Don't see the light of day,
And sometimes when people exalt
Him, he just looks away.

A gallant man takes silver out
And proudly tells the story,
How he was beaten by a snout
Deprived of gold and glory.

Silence

Let us be renewed in silence
For silence is golden,
Let us reflect with reverence
Lest we have forgotten
To be free is to be alone,
And without intrusion,
For silence is the cornerstone
Of gainful reflection.

Let us be without the treasures
That have made us remote
From fair meadows and still waters,
The little fishing boat,
And let our listening go out
To the birds in the sky,
Let the apple tree in blossom
Our spirits fortify.

Do we need to make an effort
To enjoy the sunshine?
No, just sit alone in comfort
Beneath the oak or pine,
And there listen to our breathing
Without interference,
And count that itself a blessing
In peace and in silence.

For true beauty and refinement
Rises by observing
What is already apparent
Without our dismantling,
To be alone is to be free,
Free to be hushed and still,
In silence to observe the tree
That stands upon the hill.

Everything Has its Hour

Everything has its hour to play,
Today the daffodils
Upon the ditch going my way
Gave me a thousand thrills,
In pale yellow and brilliant gold
Fluttering in the shade,
Blooming gracefully, uncontrolled
A thousand on parade.

I could not see in winters chill
A vista such as this,
For on the ditch no daffodil
Was there for me to kiss,
The ditch was bleak and cold and bare
With nothing to allure,
But now a scene beyond compare
Has won my heart for sure.

Even the old folk on the road
Are taken by the view,
They know that spring airs are abroad
Their hearts are stirred up too,
For in this panoramic scene
Their faith in life's restored,
They know that this is not routine
But inner peace explored.

Sweet daffodils of spring and hope
Great words you have inspired,
Much loved by King and Queen and Pope
By vagabond admired,
In woodland mountain vale and ditch
Everything has its hour,
Today a poor man was made rich
Dance on my special flower.

LIFE WAS A HOLIDAY

Grandad was in the eventide
Of life and growing old,
And he had many tales inside
Just waiting to be told,
So when Sue Ellen came to him
With an essay to write,
With joy he was filled to the brim
On that cold winter's night.

He told her tales about the war
When provisions were few,
Of life before the motor car,
The lack of revenue,
He knew who worked in every house
 Along the village street,
Remembered playing cat and mouse
Running round on bare feet.

She could have filled a copy book
With his muses that night,
She noticed in the inglenook
His eyes once more were bright,
Sue Ellen had her essay done
All written neat and well,
And Grandad had a heap of fun
The little girl could tell.

And then a question made him smile
That she had overlooked,
"And did you holiday in style?
Did it have to be booked?"
He looked at her bright eyes of blue
With whispered words did say,
"Life was a holiday, dear Sue,
Life was a holiday."

Thinking Back

She left her bonny baby boy
To move in with her lover,
She robbed her husband of his joy
Took ages to recover,
She had found happiness she said
To anyone who'd listen,
No more she'd put the babe to bed
That she had yet to christen.

Her new bloke gave roses and wine
Took her to the bar nightly,
Their behaviour was borderline
He kissed and held her tightly,
They flaunted their love without shame
Nor did wagging tongues matter,
And though she knew she was to blame
Her dreams no-one could shatter.

Is it not strange the way life goes?
Their love in time grew boring,
Now seldom did she get a rose
She grew tired of his snoring,
The bouncing babe is a young man
Well toned with sweet aroma,
On holiday he got a tan
In science got a diploma.

Tonight once more they're in the bar
They seldom sit together,
Her thoughts seem lost somewhere afar
She seems under the weather,
Her bloke plays pool, he's on the black
Most players he can destroy,
Up at the bar she's thinking back,
Thinking of her baby boy.

Daddy's Darling

Guess I have lost the little girl
Who used to run to me,
Who used to set my life a twirl
With fun and gaiety,
Who loved to jump up on my lap
With her new book to read,
And often woke me from my nap
For her late bottle feed.

But I have found a dazzling teen
Who keeps me on my toes,
And although she is just fourteen
I'm proud of what she knows,
She quotes her English verse so well
And loves to sit in class,
I think one day she'll teach to spell
A little boy or lass.

In years to come in fields of gold
I pray her sense of glee
Will increase by one hundred fold,
That she'll be blessed and free,
While riding the crest of a wave
She'll steer a steady course,
While knowing well how to behave
With actions and discourse.

The poem The Legend of Kumar Kuala was inspired by a visit to the Cork senior Gaelic Football team on the Saturday before the 2010 All Ireland final against Down. The team management had been looking for ways to get the team relaxed and focused for the week ahead and I was invited to speak to the players.

After my talk to the players I invited them to sing a few lines of a song with me. After a tentative start we raised the roof in Páirc Uí Chaoimh. The team adopted the chorus as their anthem for the week and with great success. The story of Kumar Kuala was read to the players the night before the final.The players were well focused and ready and won the game by one point.

I would like to dedicate the poem to the Cork team All-Ireland senior football champions of 2010.

THE LEGEND OF KUMAR KUALA
and the burning of the boats.

There is the song the natives sing while dancing hand
in hand
By the sea shore in thanksgiving for freedom in their
land;

> *'This is our island the land of our fathers'*
> *No matter where we go it's in our soul*
> *We'll fight for glory and tell the story*
> *How we won freedom for our native land'.*

How beautiful is the Fair Isle on the Pacific shore,
How friendly there the people smile with laughter in
full store,
How restful are the breaking waves that creep up on
the sand,
As bold and daring as the braves who won back their
own land,
How their forefathers lived carefree and worshiped
their own God,
And hunted on the land and sea with stick and spear
and rod,
Until the night of plunder when awoken from their
beds,
Their women were terror stricken with torch and ar-
row heads.

And children too were left to die in the huts where
they lay,
And none were left to testify at the breaking of day,
But for a few in a small boat escaped the awful deed,
And reached an isle that was remote from their own
race and creed,
A young boy at his father's side never forgot the night
His sister and his mother died without even a fight,
As he grew up he vowed one day to reclaim his own
land,
To lead his people on the way to a victory grand.

He trained himself to throw a spear fast as a shooting
star,
With an arrow to fell a deer from near or from afar,
To swim at sea, confidently jump from a running
steed,
To lead his people fearlessly by example and deed,
Down by the sea shore in the night he sat and spoke
and planned
For the moment when all would fight to reclaim their
own land,
And brothers trained their brothers who joined with
them for the cause,
And every boy to manhood grew to heartening ap-
plause.

Kumar Kuala had them trained to listen to the flow
Of water and thus was attained deep breathing
hushed and low,
And soon to him 'twas obvious their breathing was as
one,
Already in their subconscious the battle had begun,
And while they slept they dreamed a dream of palm
trees on the beach,
Of children playing in a stream, of teachers there to
teach,
They knew the day was close at hand when they
would cross the sea
And fight to reclaim their own land and set their
people free.

So when they paddled their canoes quietly o'er the
foam,
Kuala and his retinues knew they were going home,
Down by the shore for the last time they circled hand
in hand,
Kuala spoke to them in rhyme about a conquest
grand,
At first there was a gentle hum and then it louder
grew,
Just like the beating of a drum it helped those braves
anew,
The moon shone down upon the waves the chorus
louder rang,

It was the bonding of the braves and this is what they
sang;

> *This is our island the land of our fathers'*
> *No matter where we go it's in our souls,*
> *We'll fight for glory and tell the story,*
> *How we won freedom for our native land'.*

Then with a voice a clear as the water from whence
they came Kumar Kuala said;

> *This is our island-The land of our fathers'*
> *Burn the boats- For we are home'.*

Long centuries have come and gone and still they tell
the tale
About the night when called upon those brave men
did prevail,
With valour and great fortitude they raised the flag-
pole high,
Each year they dance in gratitude beneath the sum-
mer sky,
In the small huts carved out in wood, a message to
proclaim
Their hero there in brotherhood-Kumar Kuala's name,
The little boy who once had fled with his father in
fright,
Had returned to avenge the dead on the island that
night.

*This is our island- The land of our fathers'
Burn the boats- For we are home'.*

The Night the Toys Went Up
Christmas 1965

You couldn't see an elephant in our village that night
'Twas darker than a coal miner could tell,
We had to do our lessons with the help of candlelight
And Nana said I wrote my English well.
We boys were disappointed for the Christmas toys
were up
In the small shop at the end of the street,
I stood outside the window with my little doggy pup
But couldn't see a cowboy hat or treat.

We knelt down by the fire and said the rosary as one
And Granddad said 'twas cold enough to snow,
Then mother put the kettle on when the trimmings
were done
And made fresh toast beside the fireside glow.
"We don't need the electric," said my nana with some glee
Lighting another candle on the sill,
But I was seeing cowboys in my childhood fantasy
With Bobby and me riding up the hill.

I played Ludo with my Dad and before I went to bed
I put my boots and mittens by the fire,
There was Santa Clause and Christmas floating inside
my head
With every kind of plaything to desire.
My mother quenched the candle and I gazed up at

the stars
Delighted now the moon was shining through,
And I listened to the old men going home from the
bars
And thought about that window yet to view.

Oh but I was in wonderland when later I awoke
Like feathers the snow flakes were drifting down,
The men from the electric board had pulled a master
stroke
The lights were on once more in our small town.
I jumped out of my bed and crept past mam and
daddy's door
And down the stairs and out on to the street,
The snow was smooth and silky like a carpet on a
floor
The village still and sleeping sound and sweet.

I followed on small footsteps all the way down to the
shop
Bobby was there before me in a trance,
For there inside the window pane were toys you
wouldn't swap
For gold dust or a boating trip to France.
There were plastic swords and jigsaws and every type
of game
Toy soldiers all lined up behind a band,
A cowboy hat, a sheriff's badge, a green and red ball
frame

And clockwork cars that came straight from Lapland.

We sat there on the window sill; the village street was
ours
Not noticing the snow upon our brow,
And Bobby said on Christmas morn that we would
play for hours
If Santa brought a cowboy suit somehow.
We were back in our beds before the day's work had
begun
Tomorrow we'd throw snowballs on the street,
Would Santa be concerned if Granddad bought me
the new gun?
I fell asleep a new list on the sheet.

A Lesson Learned

This story I was onetime told
By Grandpa by the fire,
When I was barely nine years old
And dressed in night attire.

A warrior to heaven went
Stood at the pearly gates,
Saint Peter said you have consent
To meet the magistrates,
For you have kept the laws of God
Were brave and kind and true,
And on a rocky road you trod
When comrades they were few.

The warrior then shook his hand
But asked for one request,
Said he "that I may understand
In heaven I am blessed,
May I be shown this place called hell?
For sinners down below,
So that when I come here to dwell
Great blessings I shall know".

Saint Peter granted his request
And showed him a great room,
Where he was an invited guest
To see anguish and gloom,
To his surprise he saw in there
Fine food of every kind,
But also hunger and despair
To which folk were resigned.

The warrior said to the guide
"Why should this sad fact be?
Come tell me why they are denied
These luxuries," said he,
The guide replied "the weak and strong
Who enter hell are given
A pair of chopsticks five feet long
With which food must be eaten.

It is decreed that that they must hold
The chopsticks at the top,
The food is served on plates of gold
But see them let it drop,
For though they can pick up the fare
Their mouths they cannot reach,
And that is why you see despair
This rule they cannot breech."

The warrior was very glad
To return to heaven,
And there he saw a room which had
Tables that were laden
With edibles of every sort
As people milled around,
And they all were in great comfort
With happiness profound.

To his surprise each person used
Long chopsticks like in hell,
And he was baffled and confused
And asked the guide to tell
Him if the rules were changed up here
For each man was well fed,
"Perhaps" said he "you interfere
And feed them cakes of bread."

The guide replied "the rules don't change
Each man has the same chance,
The chopsticks must to you seem strange
And a great encumbrance,
In heaven every one succeeds
To get his fill of bread,
For when a man his neighbour feeds
Then he too will be fed."

THE SINNER

It was in the confession box
He knelt to tell his sins,
Said, "Father, I am on the rocks
I have spurned all doctrines,
It's twenty years since I have knelt
Inside the house of God,
Fraudulent were the cards I dealt
Oppressive was my rod.

Yes I have lied to God and man
And with a wicked tongue,
I've been black as a frying pan
And like a wasp I've stung,
I've robbed a pound, kept what I found
Squandered my wealth away,
I'll bet, Father, I do astound
You in this box today.

I've cursed more times than I can state
And, Father, I admit,
I've scoffed at men, sometimes with hate
Mocked those with low spirit,
I have taken God's name in vain
When on an angry turn,
And I have treated with disdain
Men who for goodness yearn.

I've been with ladies of the night
For the pleasure and thrill,
And never did I put them right
I bolted with the bill,
In alleyways with vagabonds
I have supped in the dark,
And there I waved my magic wand
Was like a patriarch.

Once I went home to see my folk
But could not venture near,
For I saw there beneath the oak
A frail man crystal clear,
It was the picture of my dad
Now tired and weak and old,
Yes, Father, regrets I have had
Since I have left the fold.

I have missed mass and I did pass
A grave where roses grow,
And dare I say like Barnabas
I betrayed friends for show,
But all the same there have been times
When I was on my knees,
Begging forgiveness for my crimes
While crying in the trees.

Yes I have cried and, Father, guess
I befriended a dog,
All skin and bone with no address
And we cut dialogue,
The funny part about it is
That mongrel made me smile,
The little that I had was his
And he made life worthwhile.

Do you think I have squared things up
O preacher of the cloth?
Could I now drink out of his cup
Be pardoned from God's wrath?
Forgive me all my sins I pray
For they displease my Lord,
That when I meet him he will say
'He came of his own accord'."

.

Unseen Glory

There's karaoke in the bar
The crowd are wild tonight,
And Johnny Macho is a star
Beneath the dancing light,
He's swaggering across the stage
While singing Status Quo,
And karaoke is the rage
In this here music show.

Alone am I amidst the throng
Of revellers in here,
And here I've sat the evening long
While downing pints of beer,
I wish that I could join the fun
And sing like Charlie Pride,
But crowds like this I always shun
I'm so fearful inside.

I've climbed a mountain, surfed a wave
And grappled with a bear,
But all the same I am a slave
To feelings of despair,
I cannot cope, I have great fear
Of facing down a crowd,
While all the others volunteer
I sit with my head bowed.

Ho-Ho there's Julianne onstage
Singing with style and verve,
She's like a model on a page
I wish I had her nerve,
With rosy lips close to the mike
She's Britney through and through,
She's all alluring, ladylike
She could be pay-per-view.

Another drink and maybe then
True courage will ignite,
Another thought of fear again
Has stalked me like a blight,
I'm weary from the ups and downs
The feeling of defeat,
The need for seeking out strange towns
Has made me obsolete.

The show is really in full swing
Who's singing "Moody Blue"?
I'll throw my hat into the ring
Requesting me to do
A Tom Jones number that I know,
"The Green Green Grass of Home",
Maybe I will go with the flow
And strike against the ohm.

My name is called out and I hide
Behind a drinking glass,
I know that part of me has died
But I vow this will pass,
Dolefully I stare at the glass
Another name is called,
But up goes Johnny bold as brass
He has the crowd enthralled.

Another drink another thought
Of demons and of fear,
For like a rabbit I am caught
Before the bright lights here,
The crowd are leaving one by one
My name is called once more,
I tell myself it is for fun
And stagger down the floor.

The words appear across the screen
I'm singing out of tune,
And yet my glory is unseen
Just like my misfortune,
The demons that have followed me
Have lost their vice-like grip,
Perhaps at last I will be free
 To pay my membership.

MARCELLA

A petite blonde Marcella was
Who pulled the pints behind the bar,
Oh she was good at it because
Folk called to her from near and far,
With ale and stout she filled them full
From early morn' till late at night,
With patience listened to their bull
Biting her lip to be polite.

The landlord of the Trapper Jacks
Upon a stool sat like a king,
Oh he was wicked with wisecracks
And let Marcella take the sting,
His jokes notoriously blue,
For the dumb blonde he didn't care,
But sat through the hullabaloo
With a Cognac- a millionaire.

She begged a rise; he wouldn't hear
Her sorry tale; she plodded on,
Only one patron shed a tear
So she struck up with her friend John,
She gave him back more dosh in change
Than ever he handed her in,
They found it easy to arrange
This collusion with discipline.

There is a bar on sunny shores
Marcella's name above the door,
She pours the drinks, he does the chores
A little girl runs round the floor,
In Trapper Jacks the pumps are dry
The landlord now is stony broke,
Still folk around there wonder why
His haughty dreams went up in smoke.

LOVE'S YOUNG DREAM

Oh that I could revisit
Love's young dream once more.

I envied so the happy pair
Who sat across the aisle,
He was handsome and debonair
She had a winsome smile,
Oh it was a pleasure to see
The twinkle in their eyes,
For they were happy and carefree
And with no special ties.

Their funny games and frolics were
Pure as the buds in May,
Nothing was going to deter
Them from their fun and play,
Together they were huddled close
Like two peas in a pod,
The young girl was her sweethearts rose
The young boy was her God.

I have known such love in my time
Back in the flush of youth,
When all things had reason and rhyme
Every word was the truth,
When every dream was plausible
While walking hand in hand,
And love as pure and natural
As footprints on the sand.

The Inter-city train sped on
Their love sealed with a kiss,
And this poor scribe was called upon
To write of love like this,
The world could have been watching there
But neither would take note,
For their young hearts were lost somewhere
In mountain, lake or boat.

Oh that true love would overcome
The obstacles of life,
Oh that true love would not succumb
To discord and to strife,
Oh that true love itself would stay
As innocent as this,
At the end of each perfect day
To be sealed with a kiss.

Right from Wrong

Confused he was by her embrace,
And by her eyes aglow,
For he saw written on her face,
"Sweetheart, I love you so,"
But still she had to go.

He bid farewell to his young son,
Said, "We'll play more tomorrow,"
Then, "Thank you, Dad, for all the fun,"
He didn't know Dad's sorrow,
That he was his to borrow.

She thought about the warm embrace,
And how she needed loving,
She'd seen the yearning on his face,
Knew he had love for giving,
And also joy for living.

Oh how they pined for what they had,
Together to belong,
Now there's a child without a Dad,
A Mum without a song,
Don't know the right from wrong.

COURAGE

It irritated me today
To walk along the beach
And watch the waves roll with their spray
A message there in each,
God calling down to teach.

But I was cluttered in my mind,
A maze without a thread,
Try as I did to leave behind
The chaos in my head,
I felt laden with lead.

Quite rueful I sat on a rock
And listened to the roar
Of the sea trying to unblock
This darkened corridor,
Her waves crashing to shore.

I stayed a while and then moved on,
The tape deck to console,
Kristofferson was called upon
To help me gain control,
On days like this when teardrops fall
It takes courage to stand up tall.

Eye off The Ball

They had the game there in their hand
Did Den and his son Jack,
For every game had gone as planned
With luck in red and black,
And one more game would win the pot
Fifty pounds each which was a lot.

Den tutored Jack on how to play
The game of forty-five,
"Eyes on the table," he would say
As to the hall they'd drive,
"And if in doubt son take your trick"
Jack noted well this rhetoric.

And all went well till the last deal
Young Jack belied his age,
As from old stagers tricks did steal
With cunning and courage,
All this while Den sat there quite chuffed
Content that Jack his chums had bluffed.

So in the all important hand
Their luck held like before,
For in Den's palm Old Nick did land
Jack held the five and more,
With trick and trump the game was theirs
Soon they would be like millionaires.

Den played the Joker into Jack
While Jack did nurse the five,
It was Jack's place to let it back
When Old Nick did arrive,
Quick on the draw like Jessie James
Father and son with fourteen games.

But as the Joker came around
Jack's eyes were fixed on Nell
The butcher's daughter who he found
Had cast him in her spell,
Not seeing who had played Old Nick
Jack thumped the table, took his trick.

The Knave was left to beat them both
Den nearly had a fit,
To leave the table he was loath
He called Jack a dimwit,
But Jack had quickly left the hall
And with Nell was having a ball!

CREATION

While resting 'neath the summer sky
I felt the hand of God close by.

The beauty of the evening sky
Made a poet of me,
For with an all embracing eye
I watched it blissfully,
The softness of the twilight glow
The hue of red and gold
Made feelings like a river flow
Through woodlands, uncontrolled.

The stillness was an unseen thread
That linked my mind and soul,
For in the half-light up ahead
The harmony was whole,
Here I was left alone in space
Where freedom is a given,
Where rich and poor man can embrace
Pure joyousness like heaven.

Even the thistles had their day
They winked at me tonight
When I looked at them in array
Their song I did recite,
They peeped out from a shady nook
Like watchmen from the ditch,
And from that corner home I took
A vista to bewitch.

Such beauty is a daily treat
For which I am beholden,
To him who gives us corn and wheat
And everything that's golden,
To the small bird that I see now
As I lay down my pen,
To sheep and lamb, to calf and cow
To creation, Amen.

Index to First Lines